BACK TO LOVING MY 1ST WIFE

A HUSBAND'S UNCONDITIONAL LOVE & THE AFTERMATH OF CAREGIVER STRESS

Written By

James Bass

CLARICE JEFFERIES

Published by Clarice Jefferies Publishing

Contact info: cjpublishing@yahoo.com

For permissions, contact:

cjpublishing@yahoo.com

**Printed in the United States of America on responsibly sourced
paper**

CLARICE JEFFERIES
PUBLISHING

Disclaimer

I am not a medical professional. Under no circumstances should the information contained herein be misconstrued as medical advice. I do not hold any qualifications or credentials in the fields of medicine, psychology, psychiatry, nursing, or any other related discipline.

The primary objective of this book is to share my journey—a narrative of affection, perseverance, and dedication. It is my testament to the lengths one may go when faced with adversity in the name of love.

Please understand the importance of seeking professional assistance when facing medical or mental health concerns. If you or someone you know is struggling with any form of illness—be it physical or mental—it is strongly advised to consult with qualified healthcare professionals.

I hope my journey resonates with you and offers insight or inspiration, it is paramount to approach the contents of this book with discernment and a clear understanding of its limitations. Remember, seeking appropriate medical guidance is crucial for addressing health-related issues effectively.

With Loving Intentions,

James Bass

TABLE OF CONTENTS

TO MY WIFE

In the kaleidoscope of life's experiences, one gem stands out above all others: the privilege of loving you. This book is a dedication to the unwavering love that binds us and a testament to my journey taking care of you.

The moment I embarked on this mission, your presence was a guiding star, illuminating the darkest corners of my world. Your smile shone brightly as the weight of responsibility fell on my shoulders, making every trial and tribulation worthwhile. Our journey was fraught with pain and tears, but your presence made even the most difficult steps bearable.

Caregiver stress was a foreign concept, but its presence became evident as I navigated the intricate dance of caring for you. Throughout it all, your resilience and unconditional love served as my anchor. Your battles were similar to mine, but your grace and strength never wavered.

Your beautiful smile became my North Star—a source of comfort and inspiration. You became my lifeline amid the difficulties, reminding me that even among the chaos of psychosis, you were still in there.

My pain and tears were real, but I am overwhelmed with gratitude as I reflect on our journey. I would walk this path again without hesitation because the honor of being your husband, caregiver, and confidant outweighs any challenges that may arise.

This book is a record of my struggle. Know that every page is infused with my passion and admiration for you. The smile that saw me through my darkest hours will live on in my heart. With my every breath,

Your Husband,

James

INTRODUCTION

For nearly three decades, I thought I knew her. I thought I understood every contour of her smile, every shadow in her eyes. But it took twenty-eight years to truly see her, to grasp the depth of the hurt she carried hidden beneath layers of armor forged by years of necessity.

As she slept soundly, I saw her differently. It wasn't just the lines etched by time on her face or the strands of silver woven through her hair; it was the unspoken weight she held, an invisible burden she bore alone for far too long.

It was as though a veil had been lifted, revealing the hurt little girl she had been carrying around. A girl who desperately needed love, validation, and safety. Then, I realized the enormity of the brick wall she had erected around herself. A fortress built not out of choice but of necessity to shield herself from a world that had been unkind.

For the first time, I saw her vulnerabilities, her fears and insecurities she had concealed so masterfully. It was like uncovering a treasure trove of emotions she had guarded fiercely, only to let me in now. And in that moment, my heart ached for her, yearning to rewrite her past, to shield her from every hurt she had ever endured.

I took honor in being the father she needed, the one who could wrap her in arms that promised safety and warmth when the world seemed cold and unforgiving. I took honor in becoming the confidant she could trust, the one she could share her deepest fears and insecurities with, knowing that my love was a shelter, no longer judgmental or dismissive.

But most of all, I found a renewed sense of purpose in being the husband she had always longed for. It wasn't just about saying the words, "I do"; it was about being the embodiment of love, resilience, and unwavering support.

I pledged to move mountains if that's what it took to see her smile again, to wipe away the traces of pain that lingered in her eyes.

It was then I realized, that despite all my shortcomings, all the mistakes and stumbles along the way, I had finally gotten something right. In a world where I had faltered and failed, I had found my purpose in loving her unconditionally. It was about walking through the fires of hell, holding her hand tightly, and never letting go until we found our way to safety.

It was challenging. Breaking down the walls my wife built took patience, understanding, and an unwavering commitment. It meant being there through the tears, the moments of vulnerability she had hidden for so long and showing her that love didn't have to come with conditions or pain.

And with each brick that fell from that towering wall, I saw her emerge, not as a broken soul, but as a survivor who had weathered storms and emerged stronger. She wasn't just my wife; she was a beacon of resilience, a testament to the power of love.

I learned to cherish every moment, to celebrate her triumphs, big and small, and to be her partner in navigating the uncertainties that life threw at us. In her, I found a strength that inspired me to be a better husband, to be the man she saw in me decades ago, when I couldn't see him myself.

So here I stand, not just proud of what I've accomplished or the battles I've won, but proud to have found my purpose in loving her; in being the husband she deserved, the father she needed, and the unwavering support she could rely on.

For in Crystal, I found the true meaning of love – a force that transcends time, mends wounds, and brings light to the darkest corners of the soul.

THE HOSPITAL DISCHARGE

I never imagined it would come to this. The hospital, the one place where you expect the best care for your loved ones, had let us down. My frustration grew as I watched my wife's condition deteriorate, and my pleas for help fell on deaf ears.

The doctors and nurses seemed more concerned with their routines rather than her well-being. They seemed to have forgotten that she was a real person, a wife, a mother, in that hospital fighting for her life.

I couldn't stay silent any longer. The weight of helplessness pushed me over the edge. Determination fueled my desire to be the advocate, caregiver, and even the makeshift doctor my wife required.

I made a decision one evening after I returned home from

visiting my wife, unable to shake the look of pain on her face from my memory. I was going to take control of the situation. If the hospital would not provide her with the care she deserved, I would. I took out my phone and dialed the hospital's front desk, and after a few transfers, I was on the phone with her treating psychiatric hospital psychiatrist.

"Hello, Dr., it's James Bass, Crystal's husband," I said, my voice firm and determined. "I need to talk to you about my wife's medication and medical care."

There was a pause at the other end, and his response was a mix of surprise and annoyance. "I assure you, Mr. Bass, that we are doing everything we can for her."

"I don't believe you are," I replied, my anger and desperation evident in my words. "I've been there every day and have seen the neglect and the differential treatment. I'm watching her mental health deteriorate. The hospital staff seems to have forgotten that my wife is a human being, deserving of more than the bare minimum."

I felt a sense of rage arising within me, an anger I'd worked hard to suppress over the years. The doctor let out a deep sigh. "Mr. Bass, I understand your concerns, but we're doing everything we can within our resources."

"I doesn't seem like it to me," I said firmly.

After a brief pause, the doctor spoke again, his tone slightly softer this time. "What exactly are you suggesting?"

"I'm taking her home," I said emphatically. "I will take care of her; I can't let her suffer any longer. I left my Family Medical Leave forms with your receptionist; I would appreciate, if you'd fill out your portion and sign them."

The doctor sighed once more and after another brief pause, he said, "I can't officially back this up, but I understand your frustration. I will fill out and sign the Family Medical Leave Form on your behalf."

Within me, a spark of hope ignited. "Thank you very much, doctor. I appreciate it."

When the conversation ended, I was filled with anxiety and determination. I knew it wasn't going to be easy. I had no formal medical training, but God had given me the strength to do what needed to be done.

Over the next few days, I worked with my HR department to file the necessary paperwork required for Family Medical Leave. It was an irritating and challenging process, but my wife's health was worth every effort.

The day finally came when I walked into the hospital, trembling but determined. Her eyes met mine, and even in her state of psychosis, I saw a glimmer of hope. "I'm taking you home," I said, my voice gentle but firm. I could feel the hospital staff's gaze on me. The young men and women in uniform exchanged disapproving glances, their eyes judging.

I could almost feel their silent scorn. To them, I was just a husband who had gone astray and was making a huge mistake. In their eyes, their training and expertise were unrivaled, and my decision was an affront to their authority. They exchanged glances and whispered behind their hands as if I didn't notice their skepticism.

But I didn't let their cynicism stop me. I filled out her discharge paperwork and signed medical forms that had become all too familiar; and as I did, I felt a surge of empowerment. I was taking charge of her care. I was going to give her the time and attention she deserved.

We walked away from the nurse's station, my wife's hand clinging to mine, leaving behind an environment that had failed her. The journey was uncertain, and I was aware of the difficulties that lay ahead. I wasn't a medical professional. I was simply a husband who refused to let his wife suffer in a place that was supposed to provide her with care.

As we passed the nurses and hospital staff, I noticed their eyes on us, a mix of curiosity, and perhaps, even a smidgeon of begrudging respect. I knew that they had a job and protocols to follow and how my actions had disrupted their routine. But I was willing to bear the burden of my decision if it meant that my wife would get the care she deserved.

I didn't have a medical degree, but I had three things more powerful—God, unconditional love, and determination.

I had no idea this journey would push me to the limits of

my abilities, putting my mental fortitude to the test. But I was prepared. I would become my wife's advocate, caregiver, and yes, even her doctor. Because when the system fails, you must step up and be the change your loved one requires.

THE BEGINNING OF "DR." BASS

I thought the worst was over when I brought Crystal home from the hospital. I had no idea that this was only the beginning of a journey that would lead me to investigate the intricate workings of her mind.

Her first few days back were a blur of sleepless nights, and confusion. I found myself tiptoeing around her, unsure how to approach the woman I'd loved for decades, who now appeared to be a stranger in her own skin. Her words were jumbled, and her emotions fluctuated between vacant stares and angry, tearful outbursts.

As I watched her struggle with her mental illness, I realized, to be there for her genuinely, I needed to educate myself. The internet became my lifeline, connecting me to invaluable resources that helped me understand the various mental health issues she was dealing with.

Night after night, day after day, I would sit at my computer, looking for answers, hoping to get a glimpse into the maze of her thoughts. PTSD, anxiety, depression, bipolar disorder, major depressive disorder, schizophrenia, and schizoaffective disorder were no longer just words, but doors to worlds of knowledge waiting to be discovered. I read countless articles, each of which shed light on a different aspect of these conditions.

The National Alliance on Mental Illness (**NAMI**) became my haven. Its pages were chock-full of expert insights and resources, making me feel less alone in this

daunting task. The stories shared by others who had previously walked this path gave me hope, assuring me that progress was possible. NAMI's articles were a "virtual support group" where I could find answers to my questions and get a grasp of this new world, I inserted myself into.

Another pearl in the sea of information was the National Institute of Mental Health (NIMH). This institution provided a wealth of research-based articles that transformed complex concepts into manageable chunks. Learning about the neurobiological bases of mental illnesses helped me understand the scientific side of what my wife was going through. The NIMH's commitment to evidence-based information gave me a sense of trustworthiness, allowing me to separate fact from fiction in a field fraught with misunderstandings.

Very Well Mind emerged as a helpful resource, offering actionable steps and strategies for navigating the daily trials that mental health conditions can bring. Their articles provided tips on symptom management, communication techniques, and self-care practices. Here, I learned the value of recognizing triggers - those subtle nuances that can set off a chain reaction of feelings and behaviors. Armed with this information, I began observing Crystal's behavior, identifying patterns that indicated when she might require additional assistance.

My commitment to understanding my wife's mental health grew stronger as the hours turned into days. It wasn't just about learning, it was about showing empathy and compassion and creating a safe space for her. I discovered that each condition had its own set of difficulties and nuances.

Her PTSD caused intense flashbacks and hyperarousal, whereas anxiety caused constant worry and physical symptoms. Depression colored her world gray, draining the joy from even the simplest pleasures.

Bipolar disorder required a delicate balance of medications and coping strategies as it oscillated between euphoric highs and crushing lows. Schizophrenia and schizoaffective disorder, although not her "official diagnosis," taught me about the complexities of psychosis, where distinguishing reality from delusion demanded a deep understanding.

The knowledge I gained from these online resources shaped my perspective and strengthened my conversations with my wife's medical professionals. With information from NAMI, NIMH, and Very Well Mind, I was able to ask informed questions, collaborate on treatment plans, and effectively advocate for her needs.

This journey was not without its difficulties. There were times when I felt frustrated and helpless, but each piece of knowledge I gained served as a beacon of hope, guiding me forward. With time, I realized that her mental illness was a part of her, but it did not define her. It was a battle she fought daily, and my role was to be by her side, armed with compassion, knowledge, and unwavering support.

In a world where psychological disorders often go unnoticed, the internet became my ally. NAMI, NIMH, and Very Well Mind provided a map through uncharted territory, arming me with the tools I needed to understand the tangled web of her thoughts and emotions. I was determined to rewrite her story, one chapter at a time, as I continued to learn and grow.

TACKLING THE DSM-5

As the weeks went by, I became consumed with researching my wife's medical conditions. Although I had countless conversations with skilled medical professionals during her hospitalization, I realized that the complexity of her condition required a deeper understanding.

I often reflected on these interactions, hoping to gain more knowledge and insight. During my reflection, I remembered a strange pattern that emerged repeatedly during these numerous discussions with her nurse practitioners, doctors, and the hospital psychiatrists. Every time they discussed her symptoms and triggers, they would pick up a particular book and flip through its pages.

I remembered how curiosity got the best of me one day during one of my meetings; I caught a glimpse of the book's title: "Diagnostic and Statistical Manual of Mental Disorders,

Fifth Edition" - the DSM-5. That was the title of the book they consulted whenever the conversation veered into the complexities of her mental state. I made a mental note to investigate this resource further, knowing that it might hold clues to the mystery of her conditions.

In my quest for knowledge, I searched the internet for information on the DSM-5. What I discovered was a detailed manual used by mental health professionals to categorize and diagnose various mental disorders. Its pages contained descriptions of symptoms, diagnostic criteria, and valuable insights into the complexities of the human mind. I ordered a digital copy of the DSM-5 without hesitation, eager to delve into its pages and grasp the nuances of my wife's mental challenges.

As soon as the book was delivered to my tablet, I began reading it. I was struck by the vast amount of information it contained. It addressed a wide range of mental illnesses, from anxiety and depression to more complex conditions such as schizophrenia and bipolar disorder. Each disorder was meticulously laid out, with detailed descriptions of the symptoms, diagnostic criteria, and potential triggers.

Reading through these pages felt like putting together a puzzle piece by piece.

I wasn't the scholarly type. College was a luxury I couldn't afford; I spent my days working hard to provide for my wife, so, words like "neuro-developmental disorders" and "schizotypal personality disorder" were unfamiliar to me. I'd never heard such complicated jargon before, and the thought of deciphering it sent shivers down my spine.

I was met with a barrage of clinical terms that felt like a foreign language. I stared at my device, frustrated and overwhelmed. My gaze darted across the paragraphs as the sentences danced around my comprehension. The words blended, and I felt like I was back in elementary school, struggling with textbooks that seemed to be written in ancient hieroglyphs.

I soldiered on for days, reading and rereading passages armed with a dictionary. I searched the internet for explanations, attempting to bridge the gap between my non-existent Ph.D. and the vast expanse of medical knowledge that lay ahead of me. Every night, after Crystal had gone to sleep, I sat at the table until the early morning hours, my brow furrowed, determined to unravel the mysteries contained within those pages.

Hours blurred into days and the gnawing frustration was relentless, threatening to crush my spirit. With each incomprehensible paragraph, the temptation to give up grew stronger, but I remembered the pain in my wife's eyes and the countless moments of confusion she had endured. I couldn't let my own limitations prevent me from supporting her.

I began to create a system, breaking down the complex language into smaller, more manageable chunks. I'd tackle each of my wife's symptoms one at a time, taking notes to help me remember the definitions and criteria. I drew diagrams, made comparisons, and talked about what I was learning to myself over and over again.

After a while, the fog began to lift gradually.

Concepts that had previously appeared impossible slowly started to make sense.

It was a triumph of endurance, a testament to the strength of willpower in the face of seemingly insurmountable odds. My understanding grew with each passing day, and I began to see the patterns and connections hidden beneath the jargon. What had appeared to be a formidable barrier had turned out to be a portal to a deeper understanding of my wife's mind.

And then it happened one evening as I sat poring over a section on schizophrenia, a concept that had eluded me for weeks, suddenly began to make sense. It was like a light bulb illuminating the darkness, casting a ray of light on the once-dangerous text. A rush of exhilaration washed over me as I realized I was decoding psychiatric jargon.

In my quest to understand my wife's mental illness, the DSM-5 proved to be an invaluable resource. Its insights broadened my knowledge and enabled me to engage more effectively with the medical professionals involved in her care. With this newfound understanding, I could participate in more meaningful conversations during meetings, ask pertinent questions, and offer observations from our daily lives at home.

The DSM-5 taught me about the complexities of mental disorders, the interplay of various factors, and the unique ways they manifested differently in people. This knowledge was not a replacement for professional expertise but a bridge that connected me to the difficulties my wife was experiencing. It enabled me to support her not only as her husband but also as someone who genuinely cared about her well-being.

Ultimately, the DSM-5 wasn't just a manual but a key that unlocked a deeper level of empathy and understanding within me. As I read, learned, and absorbed the information it provided, I was better equipped to navigate the uncharted territory of my wife's mental illness.

The book's pages became a roadmap that guided me through the complexities of her mind, and with each turn, I grew more capable of standing by her side, ready to face whatever challenges lay ahead.

SOLVING CRYSTAL'S PRESCRIPTION MEDICATION MYSTERY

E arly one morning, after one of my study sessions, I couldn't help but think about the journey my life had become. Navigating the maze of marriage was one thing, but deciphering the complexities of the medical world, a world shrouded in cryptic jargon, was an entirely different challenge.

When Crystal was diagnosed with a slew of mental health disorders, it felt like we were thrown into a storm of confusion and despair. The hospitals and pharmacies became a place of hope and trepidation, as we were handed prescriptions that held the promise of relief but also carried the weight of potential side effects and unforeseen consequences. The pills seemed to multiply like rabbits, each with its own alphabet soup of abbreviations and warnings.

The task ahead was daunting to say the least, for someone like me, who had always been more comfortable behind the wheel of a commercial truck. How could I possibly understand the jargon that had now erected a formidable barrier between Crystal's well-being and the murky depths of her medications?

Amid my desperation, I came across more online resources. MedlinePlus, Drugs.com, and WebMD became my guiding lights through the fog. Each had its

distinct approach, and their collective wisdom began to shed light on the way forward.

With its straightforward language and thorough explanations, MedlinePlus was a breath of fresh air. It appeared as if the creators were aware that not everyone navigating medical waters possessed a Ph.D. I ate up their explanations of various medications, along with disorders and conditions, licking my fingers clean while learning about their applications, side effects, and interactions. The site's straightforward design and user-friendly interface made it a reliable companion on my journey.

Drugs.com, on the other hand, felt more like a complex puzzle. It gave a thorough breakdown of each medication, from its uses and potential side effects to dosages and potential interactions. The user reviews were a mixed bag of hope and despair, cautionary tales that helped me understand the wide range of reactions to the same drugs. I was able to cross-reference medications and delve deeper into their effects using the site's search feature, providing a multi-dimensional view of my wife's treatment plan.

Despite some criticism for its commercial bias, WebMD proved invaluable in translating medical jargon into language I could understand. The articles were well-researched and approachable, explaining conditions and medications in a way that bridged the gap between the pharmacy and my mind.

The endeavor was arduous: an emotional and intellectual rollercoaster pushing my brain beyond my limits. Nonetheless, I pressed on, driven by my fierce love for my wife. Late nights were spent reading articles, cross-referencing her medications, studying symptoms and side effects, and attempting to make sense of the chemical dance taking place within her body.

The combination of the DSM-5 and resources from The National Alliance on Mental Illness, The National Institute of Mental Health, Very Well Mind, MedlinePlus and Drugs. com, enabled me to piece together a more complete picture of Crystal's condition. Armed with this knowledge, I embarked on the difficult journey of gradually weaning her off several medications that appeared to be doing more harm than good.

Nurse practitioners and hospital psychiatrists repeatedly warned me that removing medications from Crystal's care against medical advice was a dangerous path to take. They discussed potential relapses, unanticipated consequences, and a slew of risks that could devolve into chaos.

Honestly, I did hear them. Their words seared into my mind, a constant reminder of the precarious balance I was walking. But something else fueled my defiance—a love deep within me that refused to listen to their "cookie cutter" clinical advice.

I was aware of the dangers. I was aware of the high stakes. The critical difference, however, was in the foundation of my motivation. Those medical providers were motivated by their professional obligation to adhere to the protocols and guidelines established by their respective institutions. I didn't blame them; in fact, I admired and respected their knowledge and experience.

However, I carried something in my heart they couldn't fully comprehend: Love. A love that extended beyond medical records and clinical evaluations. A love that had grown greater with each shared smile, silent tear, and whispered conversation into the night. A love woven into the fabric of our marriage and developed through every storm and every ray of sunshine.

They perceived my actions as reckless, as a disregard for Crysal's safety. What they couldn't understand was that my decisions were motivated by a strong desire to see my wife whole again, free of the side effects that had trapped her. I wasn't tampering with her treatment carelessly; I was meticulously crafting a strategy fueled by my understanding of her, the knowledge of her medications, faith in God, and the tenacity of our love.

Medical science was a world of facts and statistics, probabilities and percentages. However, God defied logic, and my love was more extensive than anything that could be measured or predicted. God and love guided my every step, even when it meant going against medical advice.

With every medication I carefully tapered, with every consultation of resources and references, I became more confident, driven by forces that were both boundless and incomprehensible.

It was a deliberate and slow process, like navigating a minefield. Each reduction was met with careful observation and note-taking to ensure my wife's well-being remained a top priority. There were setbacks along the way, but perseverance and the power of love saw us through.

I held firm in the end, even as the storm of doubt raged around me. Crystal's progress was my testament—the subtle changes in her demeanor, the brighter glint in her eyes and her more freely flowing laughter and speech.

Love appeared to be a guiding light capable of illuminating even the darkest corners of our journey.

As a husband guided by God and love, I stood firm. Unmoved by the doctors that warned me against my choices. When love shines as brightly as a supernova, it has the power to reshape destinies, defy expectations, and guide you through uncharted waters to the shores of victory.

THE END OF FMLA

Six weeks had passed like the blink of an eye. As I lay in bed, watching Crystal sleep, I was struck by how quickly the days had passed since I began my Family Medical Leave. Time can be a strange thing; it is often unforgiving, but it could also be benevolent. It's been the latter in recent weeks, giving me precious moments to care for one of the most important people in my life, my wife.

When I discharged Crystal from the hospital, I knew time was critical. I made every second count. I learned to juggle tasks I never imagined myself capable of, such as cooking nutritious, delicious meals and taking on all household finances and chores, all while giving Crystal the time and attention she required.

The early days were difficult. I had to absorb information about her illness, medications, treatments, and the best ways to provide emotional support. Our home was transformed into a mini-hospital, complete with schedules, alarms, routines, and notes adorning the refrigerator. But as Crystal's mind returned, I could see the gradual improvement my care was causing.

Enrolling Crystal into an outpatient hospital program was a pivotal turning point. Transitioning from 24-hour medical care to a structured but less intensive program required a leap of faith. It was challenging to give up some control to the healthcare professionals, but I was confident that the foundation I had laid would help her thrive. The choice paid off. The program provided her with the right balance of independence and supervision, allowing her to continue her recovery.

It was nothing short of magical to watch her progress month after month. The most minor victories fueled my determination: a brighter smile, more coherent speech, a steadier gait and sparks of curiosity returning to her eyes. Each step forward demonstrated the strength of love, care, and patience.

As I lay in bed, contemplating the world outside, I knew it was time to return to work. I was grateful that the "Family and Medical Leave Act" gave me the time I needed but my heart was now engulfed in a tug of war: my devotion to my wife's well-being vs my obligation to return to work.

The morning sun cast a warm glow on the room, mirroring the optimism settling within me. Stepping back into the rhythm of the working world while still ensuring Crystal's care was going to be difficult. It would be another delicate balance, similar to the one I had mastered in recent weeks.

A sense of accomplishment swelled within me as I glanced over at Crystal, who was sleeping soundly. Her transformation was a testament to the resilience of a woman's strength and the unwavering power of God. I leaned over and kissed her forehead gently, whispering words of encouragement.

"You're going to be just fine, babe," I said softly, with a confidence that had grown over time. "I'll be heading back to work tomorrow, but that doesn't mean our journey ends here. We'll be fine, just like we always have."

Crystal slowly opened her eyes, filled with gratitude and a newfound strength. She reached for my hand and gently squeezed it. Six weeks of leave taught me that time can catalyze remarkable change when approached with care and purpose. And as I prepared to re-enter the world outside our haven, I knew that love and perseverance could bridge any gap.

We endured the storm together and remained determined to pursue the sunlight on the other side, however...

I had not fully comprehended the toll that the last six weeks, as well as the past decade, had taken on my mental state.

BACK TO THE GRIND

As I drove into the parking lot of my workplace, I felt a mix of excitement and nervousness. It was my first day back at work after taking six weeks of leave to take care of my wife. It was not an easy decision to take FMLA, but Crystal's well-being was my top priority. Walking towards the shop, I felt detached, like a puzzle piece being assembled into a half-forgotten picture.

The shop was buzzing with energy, the air filled with the aroma of motor oil and the loud sound of the air compressors. Coworkers moved through their routines, their laughter and chatter filling the space. I couldn't help but smile at how familiar everything was. During my leave, my interactions with my colleagues had been limited to text messages and sporadic phone calls. I didn't realize how I had genuinely missed their camaraderie.

Faces turned in my direction as I walked towards our locker room, and smiles lit up. A few coworkers came from the breakroom to greet me, and I was immediately surrounded by warm embraces and firm handshakes. It warmed my heart to see how happy they were to see me again.

"Hey, you're back!" exclaimed Money Mizzle, a coworker who ran our parts department. His genuine smile put me at ease right away.

"Yeah," I said, returning his grateful smile. "It's good to be back."

"How's Crystal doing?" he inquired, his concern noticeable.

"Better," my voice tinged with relief and worry. "It's been a long journey, but we're taking things one step at a time."

Mizzle nodded; his face sympathetic. "We've all been thinking about you two. Please let me know if there is anything I can do to assist."

His words were warm, and the compassion in his eyes moved me deeply. Moments like these reminded me of the bonds formed outside of the constraints of shop tasks and deadlines. As the morning progressed, I had similar conversations with other coworkers, each of whom expressed their delight at my return and genuine concern for Crystal's well-being.

Despite the heartwarming interactions, I couldn't shake an underlying sense of unease. It was as if I was wearing a coat that was too small. My mind was scattered, and despite being physically present, I found it difficult to fully immerse myself in the work environment. Tasks that used to come naturally required more mental effort, and concentration slipped through my fingers like sand.

I attributed this dissonance to the adjustment period. After all, I'd been gone for weeks, preoccupied with a role far removed from my regular automotive duties. I figured it would take a few days to re-establish my rhythm and get back into the swing of meetings and project discussions. So, I pushed through the day, directing my attention where needed and assuring myself that this was a passing feeling.

The hours seemed to fly by, and I was mentally exhausted when the clock signaled the end of the workday. Mizzle came by my bay as I was putting away my tools.

"Hey, how was your first day back?" he inquired, his voice full of interest.

I paused for a moment before offering a tired smile. "Today kicked my ass, I guess I'm just trying to shake off the rust."

Mizzle chuckled, "I understand how you feel. So, take it easy and let me know if you need anything."

"Thank you, Mizz. I appreciate you."

As I walked to my car, I reflected on the day's events. My coworkers' genuine warmth had been a balm to my soul, a reminder of the support network I had at work. However, the nagging feeling of being out of sync persisted, leaving me with a vague sense of unease.

Little did I know that this was only the beginning of a journey that would test my resilience, challenge my assumptions, and lead me down a path I could never have predicted. The first day back was just the prologue to a chapter full of surprises, the story of how a seemingly ordinary day set the stage for an extraordinary series of events that would change everything.

MY FIRST PANIC ATTACK

L ife regained some degree of normality in the weeks since I returned to work. Crystal, the love of my life, had been attending the outpatient program where I had enrolled her. Seeing her stabilize and gradually progress on her road to recovery felt good. To comply with the Covid-19 restrictions, the program had moved to virtual online meetings, and Crystal joined from the comfort of our living room. It was an odd but necessary adjustment, and she adapted just fine.

My days were a mix of work and worry, an intricate dance of responsibility and concern. Today, I found myself lying beneath a vehicle, surrounded by the complex web of wires that made up its electrical harness. The task was routine - a simple repair job demanding my focus. Yet, amid the mechanical world, an entirely different sensation began to unfold.

An overwhelming sense of urgency crawled through my veins like an invisible hand tugging at my conscience. It started as a whisper of unease but soon became louder and more persistent. My heartbeat simultaneously with it, pounding hard against my ribs and demanding my attention. As I struggled to make sense of this sudden onslaught of emotion, the world around me seemed to blur. It seemed as if I had forgotten where I was.

Sweat beads formed on my brow and trickled down my face like miniature rivers. The temperature seemed to rise, even though the cool air should have provided relief. Breathing became difficult, as if an unseen weight was pressing against my chest, constricting my lungs. It was like being smothered by a pillow in my sleep, only I was wide awake, engulfed in a nightmare created by my own body.

Instinct took over and I dragged myself from under the vehicle. With a rush of adrenaline, I thrust myself upright by gripping the rear bumper. My feet led me away from the mechanical world and into the sanctuary of our bathroom. I turned on the cold-water faucet and splashed the icy water on my face and the back of my neck.

The shock of the cold provided a brief respite, a moment of calm from the whirlwind within.

I looked at myself in the mirror, trying to figure out what had caused this sudden storm. But my own eyes were an enigma

I couldn't solve. It was as if my reflection had transformed into a stranger, a puzzle I needed to assemble amid this chaos.

Then, as if a valve had burst, tears welled up and poured down my cheeks uncontrollably.

The bathroom provided an instant disconnect from the outside world. I dashed into the first available stall, terrified that someone would barge in and see me in this vulnerable state. I shut the door behind me and sank onto the toilet lid.

I slowed my breathing as I gazed up at the ceiling. I placed my hand over my heart, trying to concentrate and match the rhythm of its beats beyond my racing thoughts. But every time I closed my eyes, an outpouring of emotion washed over me. The tears flowed freely, their source unknown, their release soothing. It was as if something within me had been opened, a flood of emotions I had suppressed for far too long.

In the isolation of that bathroom stall, I was hit by an aspect of myself I had long ignored. The weight of my worries, the strain of being the pillar of strength for Crystal, and the uncertainty of what the future held for us all converged, demanding acknowledgment. And so, I sat there, allowing my tears to mingle with the silence as the storm within slowly began to subside.

THE "EVICTION"

I marveled at the passage of time as the summer sun filtered through our living-room windows. It had been three months since I returned to work. Even as my days at the shop became more routine, a part of me still couldn't figure out why those untimely crying fits continued to occur. It was as if the emotions I thought I had tucked away were escaping at the most inconvenient times, and if that weren't enough, another surprise arrived.

It was June 1st, 2020, and it had been a day like any other day. It was late in the afternoon, and I was completing household chores when the doorbell rang, jolting me out of my routine. I sighed, half- annoyed, half-inquisitive, and made my way to the door, expecting to encounter someone trying to sell me something I didn't need.

My rehearsed dismissive greeting froze on my lips as I swung the door open. Before me stood an Asian woman with a formal demeanor. Her lips curled in a polite but genuine smile. She asked, "Mr. Bass?"

My surprise quickly turned to confusion. "That's me," I confirmed, my skepticism evident. "Can I help you?"

"I just bought this property, and I'm here to introduce myself as your new landlord." She smiled gently and handed me a white envelope. As I took the paper, my heart began pounding in my chest. "Documents regarding the new lease agreement," she explained.

I nodded, trying to keep my cool despite a storm of worry brewing. The envelope weighed heavily, not only with papers but also with the weight of uncertainty. I managed a strained thank you before closing the door softly.

I stood in the kitchen, clutching the envelope as if it held all the answers to my questions. Crystal was engrossed in her own world in the living room.

A world she was still struggling with but was determined to piece together. A world I was fierce about defending.

I opened the envelope to find a 90-day notice to vacate the property. The new landlord purchased the property using an owner-occupied loan. The loan required her to live on the premises, and out of the four units...she chose ours to reside in.

I took a deep breath and entered the living room; my voice piqued her interest. "Hey babe, I need to tell you something."

Crystal's eyes met mine, a mix of curiosity and trepidation. Concern etched lines on her face as she turned my way. I told her about the woman's visit, the ownership change, and the contents of the envelope that had turned our lives upside down.

Crystal's hands trembled as she sat on the sectional, her face a kaleidoscope of emotions. I could see her anxiety resurfacing as her eyes darted around, and her breathing became more rapid. I had to tread carefully because the last thing I wanted to do was trigger an episode.

I gently reached out, clasping her hand in mine, our fingers intertwining. Tears welled up in her eyes as she looked at me, guilt mingling with gratitude. "I'm so sorry, Daddy. I never wanted any of this to happen, especially not after everything you've done for me."

Shaking my head, I wiped away a tear falling down her cheek. "This isn't your fault babe. Remember, we're in this together. And maybe a change of scenery will be good for you, a chance to make new memories and heal." She remained quiet, unable to respond.

"Hey," I said as I held her face in my hands, "we'll get through this like we've gotten through everything else. Remember, wherever you are, that's home for me."

She nodded, her tears tinged with sadness and relief. I held her in my arms and whispered promises and comfort, determined to be the anchor she required.

I ended our conversation with a phrase I would soon take for granted during this trying time: "I'm just thankful that during this COVID-19 pandemic, I still have my job."

Unbeknownst to me...that statement would be short lived.

UNLAWFUL TERMINATION

It was now June 3ʳᵈ, 2020, two days after receiving the new landlord's notice to vacate the premises. The sun shone through my bay window, casting a dim light on my work area as I concentrated on removing bolts from the rear bumper of a vehicle.

The familiar symphony of my workspace was soothing, the hum of machinery mixed with the occasional clatter of tools, music and laughter. The world outside was temporarily forgotten as I became engrossed in the intricate dance of troubleshooting rear taillights that were non-operational.

Then, a shadow appeared over my station, breaking my concentration. Our shop manager, a portly man with a physique like Jabba the Hutt, stood there, casting an eclipse over my workspace. Along with him was his boss, a woman whose physique and facial hair cast a strong resemblance to Yosemite Sam.

"James," my manager thundered, "could you come to my office for a moment?"

I blinked; my attention drawn away from the task at hand by his request. My boss usually addressed me differently. But it was, after all, that time of year. It was the era of annual job performance evaluations and eagerly anticipated pay raises. My raises had been consistent for nearly nine years, a testament to my dedication and skill as an automotive technician.

As I walked towards his office, I felt a mixture of anticipation and nervous excitement flowing through my veins. Having secured the title of Employee of the Month for three consecutive months, being the only Certified Collision Repair Technician in the shop, having verifiable ASE (Automotive Standard of Excellence) work experience, as well as a Ford Motor Stars profile with certificates and accomplished courses ranging from automotive electronics to engine diagnostics, these were the pillars of my career. I climbed this ladder rung by rung, year after year.

But something didn't feel right as I walked into that office. The atmosphere was icy, and the way my boss and his sidekick sat—as if they were unyielding judges— starkly contrasted with the relaxed interactions we usually had during these reviews.

His voice was colder than I'd ever heard, and his words hit me like a sledgehammer. "Thank you for your years of service, James, but we are letting you go. Business is slow due to the Covid-19 pandemic."

The words echoed in my mind, shattering the mental picture I had painted moments before. The confusion washed over me like a tidal wave, quickly followed by anger and disbelief. How could this be possible? How could years of hard work and dedication be so easily dismissed?

A hurricane of angry emotions erupted within me. When my inner demons of rage and violence collided, they had the potential to unleash a torrent that threatened to consume everything in its path. My fists clenched involuntarily as I stared at him, his smug face framed by his disgustingly rotund figure. My thoughts raced as I fought to keep my old friends at bay.

As a dark and ominous cloud descended upon me, the room felt smaller and the air thicker. I struggled to take a breath, my mind raced with anguish and resentment. But there was something more to it, a knowledge that went deeper than the surface.

It wasn't the Covid-19 pandemic that had brought us to this point. It wasn't because of economic problems or business difficulties. No, it was something darker and more sinister. It was my many complaints to human resources. My complaints of the repeated use of the word "Nigger" by a co-worker, and the discriminatory, prejudiced treatment that had festered within the workplace like an ugly plague.

I was being made an example of…

I was being punished for standing up to injustice…

In the face of their prejudices, they made COVID-19 their scapegoat.

As I stood there, reeling from the blow, a part of me yearned to unleash my inner demons. To release the rage that would sever his authoritative tongue from his mouth. But reasoning, like a thin thread, held me back, reminding me of Crystal at home, who desperately needed me.

I walked out of that room, my steps heavy and my heart even heavier. The door shut behind me, sealing in the rage and agony I was feeling. My world had crumbled, and in its place was a battlefield, another new war I would have to fight. A fight for my dignity and for the change that had yet to emerge from the ashes of this injustice.

MY SHATTERED REALITY

The world around me was hazy. It was almost as if reality had slipped through my fingers, leaving me grasping at shadows. My job, the "security" it provided, and the plans Crystal and I had woven into the fabric of our lives were instantly snuffed out. The pandemic had not only claimed lives and health; it had also infiltrated the sanctity of my professional identity.

I don't recall leaving the shop. The drive home was hazy; streets I'd driven a thousand times before seemed foreign. My mind, once a fortress of order and purpose, had devolved into a battlefield littered with the wreckage of previous wars.

I sat in our driveway, staring ahead blankly. The sky was an empty blue canvas, and the day was bright. Panic rose like a tidal wave within me, threatening to drown me in its suffocating embrace. But it wasn't just about me, Crystal's delicate smile and fragile state of mind flashed before my eyes.

It had only been four months since her most recent hospitalization and only three months since I had returned to work after taking FMLA. The mounting medical bills, the cost of her therapy, her medication - it was a relentless storm. And now that I was out of work, I found myself adrift in uncharted waters, struggling to stay afloat.

My insides were gnawed by desperation. I could feel the sands of time slipping through my fingers, each grain a reminder of the unpredictability of the future. How would I pay for her hospital bills, therapy and prescriptions? How could I make sure she received the care she deserved and required? And where would we live?

As I sat in the car, drowning amid my own turmoil, I had failed to see the storm gathering within my mind. Anxiety was creeping up on me like a dark cloud.

My thoughts had taken up residence in the panic of how to care for my wife and provide for her. But it was also a fight for my sanity, against the darkness that threatened to consume me.

I exited the car, and as I stood outside our front door, the weight of the world had settled on my shoulders sinking me into a sea of uncertainty. The cold metal of the key trembled in my hand, a stark contrast to the warmth of the home we had built together. It was only a door, a barrier between me and the woman I loved, but it felt insurmountable.

I took a deep breath, my heart pounding like a drum. My mind was a raging torrent of fear and vulnerability. The news I was carrying was a dagger that I knew would pierce her heart. A gust of wind seemed to carry the weight of my hesitation away as I inserted the key and turned the lock, leaving only the raw truth behind.

Stepping inside, I softly closed the door, almost hoping the gentle click would keep reality at bay a little longer. Her footsteps approached, and I turned to see her, her eyes lighting up as she saw me. A smile began to form on her lips, and I felt my heart crack into a million pieces. How could I disrupt this moment of happiness, her face aglow with the serenity I was about to shatter?

"Hi, baby," I managed to say, my voice cracking slightly.

Her smile faded as she looked into my eyes, her intuition already identifying an issue. "What's wrong Daddy?"

I opened my mouth, but the words clung to my throat like molasses. I watched her expression shift from curiosity to concern as the storm approached. As I struggled to find the right way to tell her, her eyes widened, searching my face for answers. Then came the first tear.

Her tears flowed freely as if a dam had burst, and she stumbled back a step, her hands covering her mouth. Her sobs echoed in the empty spaces of our home as she began pacing like a caged kitten looking for an escape. As I watched her unravel, the walls seemed to close in around me, her anguish mirroring mine.

I knew I couldn't allow her to suffer. I had to regain control and redirect her thoughts. I swallowed my turmoil with every ounce of strength, pushing it down into the pit of my stomach. As she grieved, my feet moved towards her, my arms enveloping her beautiful caramel frame. The rhythm of her sobs was a painful symphony in my ears as I held her close.

"Shhh, it's okay," I said quietly, my voice as steady as possible. "I will get us through this, I promise."

I led her to the couch and sat down, pulling her onto my lap. We talked for hours, her cries fading into quiet hiccups and sighs. I assured her we were a team and that our love could withstand any storm, including this one.

With each word, I felt shivers of hope return to her body, her panic gradually replaced by a frail acceptance. Hours had passed and the darkness outside reflected the uncertainty that had engulfed our lives. And as she succumbed to exhaustion, her head nestled on my chest, I felt a bittersweet triumph.

I looked down at her while she slept, her breaths a gentle reminder that life continued despite adversity. I couldn't help but think about the near miss, how her fragile mind had teetered on the brink of something darker. But I had kept her from falling off the cliff, and that was enough for now.

I sat on the couch, still dressed in my work uniform, as the moon cast a soft glow across the room. The weight on my shoulders hadn't lifted, but in that moment, my love for her was my rock, and I was determined to ride out the storm with her, one day at a time.

REALITY SETS IN

The first week following my termination felt like a blur, like time had been thrown into disarray. My mind went into overdrive, fueled by a powerful combination of

love, anxiety, determination, and a strong sense of responsibility. The situation was far from ideal: Crystal, now four months out of the hospital, was heavily medicated and on the long road to recovery. As her primary caregiver, I knew I had to summon the strength to move forward.

The weight of reality crashed into me. With no job and Crystal's health in jeopardy, I was again faced with the daunting task of doing everything myself. However, this time, it wasn't just about keeping up with the daily chores but about securing a future for both of us. It was as if life had handed me a massive challenge, and the only way forward was to face it head-on.

But how does one find the courage to turn adversity into opportunity? How do I muster up the strength to forge ahead? I found comfort in my conversations with God, relying heavily on my belief in a higher power. It was as if God's grace had descended upon me, giving me the resilience and determination to face the storm that had unexpectedly swept into our lives.

My priority was to find us a place to live. The search for a new home became a never-ending task, a daily grind of combing through online listings, making phone calls, and touring potential residences. Reality, on the other hand, hit hard. Landlords hesitated to rent to us because I had no employment; no steady income. Rejection after rejection tried my patience, but I clung to hope and kept it moving.

A silver lining emerged amid uncertainty. My final paycheck from work, combined with my accumulated sick time and unused vacation hours, provided a significant cushion. It was a glimmer of financial relief within the darkness of our situation. I used some of the money to rent a truck and carefully moved most of our belongings into a mini storage, leaving only the essentials.

Despite the enormity of the task at hand, I approached each one methodically. I applied for unemployment compensation. My manager listed my termination as a result of COVID-19, so I was eligible for pandemic assistance through the

Unemployment Department. However, the sheer volume of applicants overwhelmed the system, leaving me in an apparent never-ending waiting game.

Days turned into weeks, and as I waited for my unemployment benefits to arrive, the gravity of our situation became apparent. Crystal's medical care and medication were critical, and I knew I needed to act quickly. Without a second thought, I made the difficult decision to sell all my company stock and deplete our 401k account to cover her medical bills and needs.

Our journey felt like an uphill battle as June turned into July. Every setback threatened to destroy my spirit. Suicidal thoughts began to creep in, but I kept reminding myself that Crystal depended on me, and I needed to be resourceful and tenacious in the face of overwhelming odds.

Those trying weeks taught me that strength is often borne of necessity. I discovered new levels of determination and courage within myself. Each setback was a lesson, and each moment of uncertainty allowed me to dig deeper. Crystal's presence, even in her frail state, served as a constant reminder of why I needed to keep forging ahead.

A RAY OF HOPE

As July wrapped its warm embrace around me, I was still locked in a never-ending pursuit of stability for Crystal. The intensity of my search for a new place to live and a job that would serve as a lifeboat in the stormy sea of financial uncertainty was mirrored in the intensity of the summer sun.

As I scoured online job listings, filled out applications, and submitted resumes, the days seemed to fly by. Crystal, whose smile had always been my pillar of strength, was the only thing that kept my spirits alive. The looming shadows of her medical bills threatened to swallow us whole. But I held her up and pressed on.

Meeting after meeting with landlords who seemed more interested in my job loss than in my humanity left me disheartened. We trudged around to look at apartments that were far from our ideal. I recall the expressions of those who turned us down, each rejection was a bitter pill to swallow. However, as the adage goes, it is frequently darkest before dawn.

A phone call changed everything just when I thought hope was slipping through my fingers. A landlord with a kind and sympathetic voice was willing to give us a chance. He had a small one-bedroom, one-bathroom apartment available, it lacked the luxurious amenities we once took for granted but it offered us something far more valuable: a roof over our heads and a chance to rebuild.

It wasn't a lot. There was no attached garage, no indoor laundry, no fireplace, and it had no room for our treadmill or gym equipment. But the moment we stepped into that humble apartment; its walls seemed to reverberate with the promise of a new beginning. Crystal's tired smile was visible as she looked around, her eyes reflecting the gratitude that filled our hearts.

We moved our few belongings into our new home with renewed purpose. Then, just a few days later, I got the call I'd been waiting for; a potential employer was interested in interviewing me.

As I prepared for that pivotal moment, my heart raced with a mixture of excitement and anxiety.

The interview was nerve-racking, but I felt a glimmer of hope as I walked out of the office. I had no idea this glimmer would soon transform into a radiant beam. A few hours later, I received a job offer, along with the information that, while the

pay was slightly lower than my previous position, it came with a valuable perk: comprehensive medical benefits. The weight of worry that had been pressing against my chest suddenly dissipated. My wife's mental health would be taken care of, which was a victory in and of itself.

A wave of relief washed over me as we settled into our new apartment. The storm had finally passed; the cloud of uncertainty had given way to a clear sky…but…

As life frequently shows, triumphs can be deceptive, masking internal battles. The newfound stability I had worked so hard to achieve became a breeding ground for a different kind of struggle - one that couldn't be solved with a lease, or a job offer. I was unaware of an insidious darkness encroaching on my thoughts and emotions.

The journey that began with determination and hope was taking an unexpected turn, which I was unprepared for. Shadows that used to loom on the horizon now seemed to dwell within me, gnawing at the edges of my sanity.

Little did I know that this triumphant time would herald the start of a different kind of battle - a battle for my own mental health.

My First Mind Slip

We moved into our new one-bedroom apartment at the beginning of August 2020, and we were very grateful to have found stability there. After the moving puzzle had finally come together, my attention went to getting ready for a new chapter— my first day at a new job. I was about to step into the role of Commercial Residential Driver for a waste management company.

The night before had been a blur of excitement and nervousness. I carefully gathered my work clothes, boots, and lunch, ensuring everything was in its proper place. But my preparations went beyond just myself; I prepared Crystal's medication and I set an alarm clock to chime four times a day. I knew I wouldn't be there to remind her, and her state of health was constantly on my mind.

As I lay in bed, sleep eluded me. The anticipation of a new job was mixed with a pressing concern for Crystal's well-being. Every creak in the walls seemed to amplify my feelings.

Morning came too quickly, and as I stood up to greet the day, I couldn't shake the feeling that something wasn't quite right. Perhaps it resulted from stress and lack of sleep, but I felt a persistent unease in the pit of my stomach. I ignored the sensation and dressed for work. I kissed Crystal goodbye while she slept and whispered, "I love you." I assured her that I'd be back before she knew it.

I double-checked my list: boots, gloves, lunch, and medications before heading out the door. The sky was still draped in the quiet of darkness, and the world around me seemed to exist in a haze as I drove to work. It was as if my consciousness was detached and watching my actions from afar.

At 4 a.m., I arrived at the waste management company and reported to my trainer, a seasoned driver who exuded confidence and experience. He walked me through the morning routine and explained the intricacies of the job. But I was having trouble keeping up with his words.

It was as if my mind was engulfed in a thick fog, making it difficult to process information that was usually second nature to me.

We were soon on our way, the rumble of the truck beneath me a constant reminder of my new reality. The trainer's voice came over from the driver's seat, words jumbled together. I had to concentrate like never before, straining to catch each word as if they were fragments of a foreign language.

Hours passed like seconds, and soon it was 8:30 a.m., time for our lunch break. I took out my cell phone as the trainer pulled into a gas station and exited the truck to get a drink. I intended to call Crystal, to hear her voice and offer solace amid my mental chaos. But a surreal sensation washed over me as I stared at my phone's screen. I struggled to recall the name attached to her phone number.

My heart raced, and at that moment, I realized that something was deeply wrong. The sensation of being "off" was not just a result of lack of sleep; it was something more profound, something that touched the core of my being. As the puzzle pieces shifted, a chilling realization dawned – my mental faculties were betraying me.

MY SECOND MIND SLIP

It's strange how the mind can deceive you and transform the simplest tasks into a mind-bending puzzle, a labyrinth of perplexity. For years, I took pride in my sharp memory and ability to recall details without hesitation. But, staring at the contact list on my phone screen that day, I felt I was drowning in a sea of digits.

Crystal's phone, which I had called a thousand times before, seemed foreign to me. Panic clawed at the edges of my awareness, my mind a blank canvas splattered with worried brushstrokes. I blinked hard, wanting my phone's contact list to make sense, but the words danced and twisted in front of my eyes, refusing to form the familiar name attached to her number.

My trainer returned to the truck as I stood frozen. He was explaining some of the finer points of the job, but his words were just background noise. I slipped my phone back into my pocket, pretending nothing bothered me. My confusion, however, weighed heavily on my chest.

As my anxiety grew, he continued to ramble on, his words forming a barrier between us. I nodded at the appropriate moments, chuckled a few times, and prayed that my mask did not slip. The minutes seemed to stretch on forever, a never-ending cycle of pretending, until the break ended, and we returned to work.

The trainer handed me the route sheet, a list of streets and addresses I was required to learn. I'd been a commercial driver on and off for over a decade and Fresno was etched in my mind. My professional driving career began in 1994 and I knew my streets like the back of my hand.

But as I took the route sheet from the trainer, a sharp panic sliced through me; none of the street names, let alone the addresses, were familiar to me. My heart was racing, as I flipped through the pages quickly, my fingers trembling as I tried to understand what I was reading.

 But it was pointless. The addresses were like hieroglyphs, and the streets were like blank paths.

"Hey man, you good?"

My frantic thoughts were cut short by the trainer's voice. I jerked awake, the weight of his gaze on me. My mind raced to come up with an explanation for my behavior.

"Yeah, I'm fine," I said, my voice steady, though my heart continued to thud erratically. "Just a lot of stops along the way."

The response was adequate. The trainer smiled sympathetically and chuckled. "Yeah, and believe it or not, today is a light day." We laughed together, but I couldn't get rid of the nagging feeling that something was wrong.

I kept my unease hidden beneath layers of professionalism as we continued our journey. But it was difficult to ignore the nagging doubt that had taken root. What was going on with me? How could I have forgotten streets I'd known since childhood? I couldn't get rid of the feeling that this was more than just a lapse in memory.

As the day wore on, I couldn't help but wonder if something deeper was at play, something lurking in the shadows of my thoughts. And as the city I thought I knew so well stretched out before me; I couldn't escape the feeling that I was a stranger in my hometown.

ALL IS FORGOTTEN

As I sat in the truck's passenger seat, the monotony of the road ahead seemed to blur into a surreal landscape. My mind was a cloudy labyrinth where thoughts seemed to dissolve before I could grasp them. My memory seemed to slip through my fingers like gravel. My trainer was babbling about the complexities of our job, but his words were becoming incomprehensible. I nodded and smiled, pretending to understand despite my mind teetering on the edge.

Then, the worst came crashing down. We turned a corner, and the surroundings that had been imprinted on my mind since childhood seemed strange. I was in my hometown, where I grew up, lived, and loved, but I felt like a stranger in unfamiliar territory. Panic began to rise in my throat, constricting my breathing. I stared at the cityscape, at the familiar landmarks that should have guided me, but they were like jumbled puzzle pieces that refused to fit together.

I looked up, my gaze fixed on the road ahead and the mountains' distant outline. I'd used these landmarks to orient myself, to know which way was north and which was south. But now everything was a disorienting blur. My palms became clammy as I grappled with reality slipping through my fingers.

Desperation ripped at my heart, but I needed to maintain a calm demeanor to appear normal. I couldn't tell my trainer that I was becoming disoriented. I inhaled slowly and deliberately, each inhalation an attempt to ground myself in the present moment. But the more I tried to reorient myself, the more the world seemed to tilt on its axis.

The freeway on ramp loomed ahead, and my trainer merged onto it, the steady hum of the engine providing a backdrop to my inner turmoil. We were going to the city dump, a place I had not been to since childhood and the minutes stretched like elastic as we drove. Then, gradually, a flash of recognition broke through the fog.

The city landfill appeared, its towering mounds of garbage providing an odd sort of comfort. I now realized where I was, about 12 miles from home. The realization weighed heavily on me as I tried to understand what had just happened.

My hand shook as I reached into my pocket for my cell phone. Crystal's psychologist, Dr. Marchita Masters, was saved in my contacts. With shaky fingers, I texted out a message, the words reflecting my vulnerability. *"Dr. Masters, something isn't right. I need your assistance,"* I typed, my fingers stumbling over the keys.

I took a deep breath and pressed the send button, as if sending the message would free me from the grip of the inexplicable turmoil that had consumed me. The phone felt heavy in my grip, like a lifeline stretching into the unknown. As we drove down the highway, my gaze remained fixed on the screen, hoping for a response that would shed light on the perplexing abyss that had opened within me.

My heart raced after I sent the text message, and time seemed to slow to a crawl. My worries pressed heavily against my chest, and I couldn't help but wonder if asking for help was the right thing to do.

A soft ping from my phone finally jolted me out of my reverie. As I read her response, my heart skipped a beat, *"What's going on?"* These three simple words held the promise of direction and comprehension. I typed back with shaky fingers, my thumbs clumsily tapping the screen.

"I'm not sure. Something isn't right. I'm at work right now, and I'm having trouble remembering. For a moment, I became disoriented, and I had no idea where I was."

The minutes that followed felt interminable as I awaited her next message. The seconds between my text and her response seemed to stretch indefinitely, filled with uncertainty and fear.

Her reply came in like a lifeline. *"What time do you get off work?"*

A ray of hope broke through the fog of uncertainty. I replied as quickly as I could, my fingers struggling across the screen, *"I'm not sure."*

Her following message was brief and to the point, *"Call me as soon as you clock out and are on your way home."* Her words guided me to shore like a lighthouse in a stormy sea. I quickly typed *"Thank you,"* and slipped the phone back into my pocket.

The rest of the 12-hour workday passed in silence. My mind was consumed by worries and questions, making it difficult to focus on my tasks. My trainer's voice was a distant echo, and even the familiar hum of the engine seemed distant and unreal. It was as if I were trapped in a bizarre dream, a haze that wouldn't lift.

Finally, we pulled back into the yard at the end of the day. The digital clock on the wall struck the appointed hour, and I clocked out. The relief was tangible, like shedding a heavy coat I hadn't realized I'd been wearing. The silence enveloped me as I settled into my car and shut the door.

In that moment of solitude, everything came crashing down on me. As I gripped the steering wheel, tears welled up in my eyes, blurring my vision. I put my head down and sobbed uncontrollably as the floodgates opened. I cried because I didn't know what the future held and was frustrated by my lack of direction. I cried because I was filled with fear, confusion, and vulnerability, all of which had become my constant companions.

As the tears dried, a sense of determination took their place. Dr. Masters instructions provided the necessary anchor, assuring me I would not have to navigate this journey alone. I wiped my tears away and pulled out my phone, dialing her number with renewed resolve. It was time to take the first step toward understanding and healing, regardless of the uncertain road ahead.

DR. MARCHITA MASTERS

It wasn't long before Dr. Masters picked up the phone. The soothing sound of her voice washed over me, providing comfort and assurance in a time of great uncertainty.

"Hey, James, can you tell me what's going on?" Her gentle tone was like a lifeline thrown to a drowning man.

I never imagined I'd be seeking help from Dr. Masters, a psychologist I had initially sought out for Crystal. She was an extraordinary woman. A warm, compassionate and nurturing soul. Along with her 33 years of experience and impressive credentials: a Bachelor of Arts in Psychology, a Master's Degree in Psychology, and a Psy.D. in Psychology - were overshadowed by her genuine humility and love for her profession.

"Hey, Dr. Masters," I said, my voice shaking. "I'm not sure what's going on with me. My brain has turned to mush. It's difficult for me to concentrate and focus on the most basic activities. I couldn't remember Crystal's phone number earlier, and then I got lost, not knowing where I was."

Tears welled up again as I expressed my confusion and fears, blurring my vision as I listened to Dr. Masters. Her compassion and understanding poured through the phone like a warm embrace.

She didn't waste any time. "James, do not return to work tomorrow. You're not fit to work, let alone drive a commercial vehicle."

Her words were heavy with concern and a deep sense of responsibility. This wasn't the first time we'd discussed it. I had been on the verge of a mental collapse a year before, caught in the whirlwind of caring for Crystal during her terrifying episodes of psychosis.

Dr. Masters had warned me about the dangers of ignoring my sanity. She admired how I looked after Crystal, putting her needs ahead of mine.

But she also warned that by doing so, my mental health and stamina would eventually deteriorate.

Her voice had taken on a new urgency. "I'm declaring you unfit for work and I'm placing you on temporary leave. You must concentrate on your health. The human mind can only handle so much stress, especially when caring for someone you love."

Her words were both a verdict and a lifeline. She was more than just a psychologist; she was a friend and a guide through the darkest times of my life. As I listened to her, I realized that seeking assistance was not a sign of weakness but rather an act of self-preservation. Dr. Masters had a way of making even the most difficult decisions seem apparent.

"Thank you, Dr. Masters," I said quietly through my tears. "I appreciate you."

She assured me we would work through this together as we had previously done with Crystal, and she scheduled me an appointment for the following day. I found solace in her wisdom and compassion amid my turmoil. Dr. Masters was more than a doctor; she was an anchor that kept me from drifting into the abyss.

CHECKING MY EGO

The thought of not working gnawed at me like an itch. It was as if my very identity, my very essence, was entwined with the idea of earning a living with my bare hands. I had always taken pride in being the provider, supporting my wife, and keeping our household running smoothly. The thought of relying on the "system" for a paycheck felt strange and unsettling, like a betrayal of everything I had worked so hard for.

However, Dr. Masters was a wise woman with a gentle demeanor. She had a way of making you feel heard even when you were struggling to express yourself. She finally got me to open up about the unrest I felt about not working.

"James," she said, her voice soothing my frazzled nerves, "I understand your apprehension about disability benefits, but I want you to know that these are *your* benefits. You've been contributing to the system since your first paycheck. It's not a handout; it's a safety net."

I shifted in my seat uncomfortably, unable to shake the sense of guilt that washed over me. "Dr. Masters, I've always been the one who takes care of things. The idea of not working, of relying on others, does not sit well with me."

She responded thoughtfully. "I admire your commitment and sense of responsibility. But the most important thing right now is your mental health. You've been carrying a heavy load for a long time, and it's taken its toll."

My fingers fidgeted with the seam of my pants as I looked down at my hands. "I feel like a loser."

"You're not a loser, James." Dr. Masters responded. "You're a man who needs help, just like anyone else; you've given so much of yourself to Crystal; now it's time to treat yourself with the respect and care you deserve."

Her words struck me, but the fear of being judged lingered. "How will people perceive me?" "What will my boss think when he finds out I went on disability after just one day of work?"

She reassured me, "What matters most, James, is your health. And, once again, disability benefits do not reflect your worth or abilities. They are specifically designed for situations like yours, to provide the assistance you require when confronted with health difficulties."

A wave of relief washed over me as I listened to her. Dr. Masters had a way of breaking down my barriers and helping me see things in a new light. She was correct; my stubborn pride and fear of being judged had held me back for far too long. It was time to put my mental health first, even if it meant temporarily relying on disability benefits.

"But what am I going to do while I'm on disability?" My mind raced with possibilities and doubts as I inquired.

Dr. Masters took a brief pause. "Well, this is your chance to focus on yourself, to heal and regain your mental strength. It does not imply that you must remain idle. Along with using this time for therapy, you can also pursue hobbies and interests that bring joy to your life."

I nodded slowly, taking in what she was saying. It was a fresh perspective, an opportunity to refocus my efforts on self-improvement. It was, however, a frightening step into the unknown.

"I know it's not an easy decision," Dr. Masters said, her voice filled with empathy. "However, remember that your mental health is your most valuable asset. You're investing in your future, stepping into your ability to be the best version of yourself for your wife and your well-being."

I thanked Dr. Masters as our video session ended, a mix of emotions swirling inside me. The prospect of not working still bothered me, but her wise and empathetic advice planted hope in my heart.

It was time to let go of the stigma and misconceptions about disability benefits and embrace them as a lifeline during this difficult time in my life.

Looking out my living room window, I couldn't help but consider the positive possibilities of this unexpected break in my life. It could lead to a healthier and happier future, where I finally prioritize my well-being and regain the peace of mind, I had lost…However, I greatly underestimated how much my mind had been affected.

FURTHERING MY EDUCATION

When Dr. Masters suggested I find a way to keep my mind occupied by pursuing hobbies or interests, I didn't take it seriously. "You need to find something productive to do," she said. "It'll help with the stress and give you a sense of purpose." I nodded and smiled, but in my mind, I thought, "Yeah, right. Like I have time for hobbies."

Taking care of Crystal was a full-time job. The thought of adding anything else to my plate seemed laughable. But as the days turned into weeks and the weight of her illness bore down on both of us, I started to see the wisdom in Dr. Masters' advice. The more I thought about it, the more I realized that I wasn't just burning out—I was also falling into a kind of intellectual stagnation.

Crystal and I had always shared a love for learning. Before she got sick, we'd spend our evenings discussing documentaries we'd watched. Our home was filled with books on every conceivable subject. Now, I barely have the energy to read a magazine, let alone dive into a new topic. My mind constantly raced with worry, leaving little room for anything else.

As I reflected on Dr. Masters' suggestions, I realized that the websites and online forums would only get me so far; I came to a profound realization: if I truly wanted to support Crystal through her mental health struggles, I needed to educate myself properly. Her battle with psychosis was unlike anything I'd encountered before, and I needed to be better equipped to help her. However, the traditional route of registering and attending college wasn't feasible for me. My wife required constant attention, and I was grappling with my own mental health challenges as well.

By sheer luck, I stumbled upon information for online courses from Penn Foster College and Harvard Health Publishing Harvard Medical School. Intrigued, I visited Penn Foster Online first, eager to see if they had something that could help me.

To my surprise and relief, they offered various courses that seemed ideally suited to my needs. I signed up for four courses immediately. The first course I chose was Professional Communication Skills. I needed to improve my ability to communicate not only with my wife but also with the voices that communicated with her. This course was a game-changer, providing me with techniques to engage in more meaningful and effective conversations, ensuring that I could be a calming and supportive presence for her.

Next, I enrolled in two courses, Managing Personal Health and Managing Stress. These courses helped me identify and manage the stressful situations that could trigger Crystal's episodes. I learned how to create a more serene environment for her and cope with my stress, which was crucial for our well-being.

The last Penn Foster course was Positive Relationships in the Workplace. Although it was designed for professional settings, I realized I could adapt the principles to my home life. By thinking of my interactions with Crystal in terms of workplace relationships, I learned how to navigate the various "roles" she inhabited during her episodes. This course taught me to maintain positivity and patience, which was essential for our marriage.

After completing these courses and proudly obtaining my certificates, I turned my attention to Harvard Health Publishing Harvard Medical School. Their courses offered more profound insights into mental health, which was exactly what I needed.

I paid my fees and enrolled in two courses: Understanding Depression and Positive Psychology.

Understanding Depression provided me with a comprehensive view of the condition, helping me grasp what my wife was experiencing on a daily basis. This knowledge enabled me to be more empathetic and supportive.

Positive Psychology, on the other hand, equipped me with strategies to uplift her spirits and foster a more positive outlook. It taught me the importance of small, consistent actions that could make a significant difference in her mental health.

These six courses taught me a wealth of knowledge and skills that transformed how I supported Crystal. The education I received online was not just academic; it was practical and directly applicable to our lives. It empowered me to be a better husband and caregiver, and most importantly, it gave me hope. We still had our challenging days, but now I was armed with understanding and a toolkit of strategies to navigate the complexities of mental illness.

ENTERING THE HAZE OF MADNESS

In my first book, "In Love with My 5 Wives: A Broken Man's Journey on How to Love His Broken Wife," I share the highs and lows of my turbulent journey throughout my childhood, young adult life and marriage. Chapter 30 stands out as a testament to one of my darkest moments, a chapter I wouldn't wish on anyone, not even my worst enemy.

In this chapter, I delved deep into my wife's battle with psychosis, a harrowing experience that tested the boundaries of my love, compassion, and mental fortitude. Her symptoms were disturbing, a swirling maelstrom of confusion, paranoia, and hallucinations that rocked the foundation of our marriage.

I should clarify that my wife doesn't remember much of what happened during those turbulent times. Psychosis is a cruel illness, robbing its victims of their memories, their grasp on reality, and, in many cases, their sense of self. But unfortunately, I remember everything. I was there through it all, a participating witness to the horrors that played out inside her head.

As I write these words, I remember a saying: ***"There are some things the mind cannot unsee."*** I witnessed those events and lived through them, and they left indelible scars on my psyche. It's a burden I'm still carrying.

Dr. Masters became our beacon of hope during that time. However, in my case, it brought forth a unique dilemma. Crystal, the very subject of my therapeutic endeavors, was prohibited from participating in my sessions.

The reasons were dire and unavoidable. My discussions with Dr. Masters delved into the most disturbing aspects of our shared experience. Psychosis, paranoia, and nightmarish hallucinations were not topics suitable to bring up in front of Crystal. It wasn't just to save her from the agony of remembering those atrocities; it was also to protect her fragile mental state, to prevent any possible triggers that would cause her to have a relapse of symptoms.

The threat of post-traumatic stress disorder (PTSD) loomed over us. Even the slightest trigger could send her spiraling back into psychosis. The thought of witnessing her go through that agony again was a nightmare I couldn't bear.

So, with Dr. Masters, I faced each therapy session alone, navigating the labyrinthine recesses of our shared suffering. It was a complex and emotionally draining process that required me to confront my inner demons. I was determined to be the rock my wife needed, to comprehend her journey and how it had shaped the woman I adored.

In the following chapters, my story takes a darker turn, a descent into the realm of madness that may disturb you. These are not words for the faint of heart, as I embark on a journey into the unknown, hoping to emerge stronger.

Know that my goal in recounting my journey is not to shock or harm you but to shed light on the reality of mental illness and the power of love in its face. I hope that by sharing my experience, I will be able to assist other men who may be navigating similar treacherous waters.

So, proceed with caution, and remember that even in the depths of despair, there can be resilience, redemption, and a love that knows no bounds. My journey is a

testament to that enduring love, and I invite you to join me as I seek healing, understanding, and ultimately, a love that conquers all.

SLEEPLESS NIGHTS

The days had become a never-ending loop of despair. When Dr. Masters originally suggested that I take some time off work to relax and focus on improving, I thought it would relieve my tortured soul. I had no idea that leaving my job would simply exacerbate the constant anguish that had taken up residency in my head.

When caring for Crystal, I lost around four to five hours of sleep every night. But now, I'm losing entire days of sleep. I find myself staying awake for two, three, and sometimes four days at a time. I am locked in a constant battle with the chaos brewing within my mind, unable to find peace in the embrace of sleep. And when my body finally succumbs to pure exhaustion, I sleep for only a few hours before being rudely awakened by the never-ending turmoil in my head.

Dr. Masters recommended that I incorporate exercise activities into my daily routine, such as lifting weights, going for a brisk walk, or even hitting the punching bag, as I used to. But the truth was that I didn't want to do anything. I couldn't escape the sorrow that clung to me like a shadow. I told Dr. Masters that I didn't have it in me anymore and that I couldn't stop crying.

She asked me to elaborate, so I did. I told her that I cried uncontrollably at night while my wife slept peacefully beside me. I didn't want to wake her up with my constant sobbing, tossing and turning, so I'd seek refuge in the living room. I'd sit alone in the dark, my heart heavy and my tears falling quietly.

Music, which had once brought me joy, became a source of my tears. I couldn't stand listening to songs that reminded me of happier times spent with Crystal. Even some commercials, with their soft melodies and heartfelt scenes, had the power to move me to tears. I used to mock these "cheesy" commercials for their feelings of affection, and now, I cry when I see them.

My constant sobbing had given way to rage. A rage I worked so hard to control was now simmering beneath the surface, ready to erupt at the slightest provocation. I became increasingly irritable, unable to control my temper. I had begun snapping at Crystal over trivial matters that were not her fault. My growing frustration was eroding my love and compassion for her, which only fueled my despair.

Dr. Masters listened patiently as I poured out my heart to her, her eyes filled with understanding. She began to speak after I had finally revealed the depth of my anguish, her voice calm and reassuring.

"What you're experiencing," she began, "are symptoms of depression. Your rage, irritability, impatience, difficulty sleeping, and constant tears are all symptoms of this emotional storm."

I sat listening, my heart heavy but eager for answers.

"You've been a pillar of strength and a rock of support for your wife," she continued.

"A lot of bad things have happened to you in a short period of time, and you've suppressed a lot of your emotions to move forward. It's unpleasant, but you'll soon feel like your old self again."

Dr. Masters' words were soothing to my mind and spirit. They provided a glimmer of hope that I might one day be able to find my way out of the darkness that had consumed me. At the time, I clung to her advice, a promise of a way back to the light.

Dr. Masters outlined a plan for my recovery as we talked. Individual therapy for now and couples therapy was on the horizon. She mentioned the idea of seeing a psychiatrist for medication as a possibility to help stabilize my mood and improve my sleep. Most importantly, she assured me I would not have to bear this burden alone; she would be by my side every step of the way.

I felt a glimmer of hope as we finished our video session that day. The road ahead was still dark, but now I had a guiding light to lead me through it.

THE SHADOWS

The days were now blurring into a sleepless haze. My body and mind were taking a toll from the lack of sleep, and my reality would soon begin to fracture.

I dismissed it at first as fatigue-induced hallucinations, a fleeting trick of the light, a shadowy flicker in my peripheral vision. However, these strange apparitions became more frequent, substantial and infinitely disturbing as the weeks progressed.

I blamed the sightings on my chronic insomnia. After all, sleepless nights had a way of playing tricks on the mind. I brushed it off, thinking it was just a side effect of my sleep-deprived lifestyle. Plus, I had learned of such delusions while learning about and caring for Crystal during her battles with psychosis.

However, I started to notice a pattern. These enigmatic forms, dark and elusive, would only appear in the late evening. A gentle sense of relief would wash over me as the morning slowly came, as if the sun's soothing rays could chase them away. I still clung to the idea that my lack of sleep was to blame, that my overworked mind was conjuring these apparitions.

Nonetheless, their presence became more obtrusive over time. These spectral figures ventured forth, now manifesting themselves in broad daylight. They were lurking in the kitchen corners, the recesses of the living room and in the corners of our bedroom. When I turned to confront them, they no longer floated away with a quick disappearance. Instead, they lingered for agonizing moments, dancing on the edge of my vision before fading away.

The size of these dark entities grew in conjunction with the evening's darkness. What had once been mere flickers had grown into looming, menacing figures. They moved hunched over, ensuring their shadowy heads didn't scrape the ceiling.

I couldn't bring myself to tell Crystal about my newfound agony. She slept soundly beside me, blissfully unaware of the shadows that stalked my every waking moment. I was afraid that revealing my growing paranoia would trigger her symptoms, and I couldn't bear the thought of burdening her with my condition.

As the nights passed, I retreated further into the abyss of my sleepless existence. In a desperate attempt to flee these menacing apparitions, I sought refuge in the murky darkness. I started spending my nights alone in the living room, where the shroud of darkness provided my only shelter. I could finally get away from the sinister presence that was taunting me.

My reprieve, however, was brief. The shadows became more prominent in the absence of light. They surrounded me, closing in on all sides, their obsidian forms dancing on the rim of my vision. Their malicious intent was perceptible, a presence that seeped into my very soul.

The loneliness became unbearable. I was a prisoner in my own home, tethered by the chains of my sleepless nights and the constant torment of these shadows. Fear clutched at me, its icy fingers tightening with each passing second. I was unsure of how much more I could endure this unbearable silence.

SHADOWS BECOME HEADLESS, FACELESS PEOPLE

I recall the first time it happened, when I first saw them. It appeared to be an ordinary day in our tiny apartment. Sunlight filtered through the blinds, casting long shadows across our living room. Crystal was asleep beside me in her recliner, her breath slow and steady.

It started as a subtle flicker in the corner of my vision, which I once again dismissed as a trick of my tired mind. But as I stared at the living room wall, the flicker became more intense. I couldn't take my eyes off the shapes moving in the shadows. The longer I stared, the more transparent they became—silhouettes, faceless and hazy.

These shadows, which first appeared at night, would walk back and forth just beyond my awareness, barely brushing the edge of my perception. They seemed lost, looking for something that could never be found. They shuffled, stumbled, and swayed, mocking me with every move.

I recall one day vividly. The dim sunlight cast eerie patterns on our kitchen blinds, creating a distorted, dancing silhouette. I convinced myself that someone outside was disoriented or lost, possibly a delivery driver searching for the correct apartment number. I felt a surge of concern, my heart racing, as I considered offering assistance.

I rose slowly from my seat, trying not to wake Crystal. The linoleum floor creaked softly beneath my weight as I approached the kitchen window. Outside, a mechanical figure moved back and forth. My breath caught in my throat as I reached for the blinds and pulled them apart.

There was a faceless figure standing just beyond the glass. It had black skin, limbs that stretched unnaturally long, and wore tattered clothing that blended into the shadows. Its hollow eyes stared at me, even though it had no eyes to see with. I stumbled back, tripping over my own feet as my heart pounded in my chest.

I slammed the blinds shut and covered my eyes with trembling hands, still trying to understand what I had just seen. My mind raced, looking for a logical explanation.

However, there was none. I couldn't shake the feeling that I'd witnessed something out of this world, something that defied logic.

"What happened, Daddy?" Crystal asked as she stirred in her seat, her voice groggy.

I quickly wiped the tears away from my eyes and swallowed hard, my voice shaky but composed. "It's not much babe, I thought I was going to sneeze, but it went away."

She mumbled something back, her breathing returning to normal. As I returned to my seat beside her, the weight of the encounter was pressing against my chest. The faceless figure haunted my thoughts as I sat in our fully lit living room.

The faceless figures became a daily occurrence as the weeks passed. They were no longer confined to the shadows outside our apartment. Instead, they approached with frightening boldness, crossing the threshold of our home.

I'd wake up in the middle of the night to find them in our hallway, their featureless heads slowly turning back and forth. Their movements were jerky, like marionettes controlled by a malevolent force. They were my jailers, and the apartment felt like a prison.

I couldn't take it anymore one night. I summoned the courage to confront one of them outside our bedroom door. It was a figure with no head, a void where its neck should have been. I cautiously approached it, its body swayed as if suspended by invisible strings.

"What do you want?" I demanded, my voice trembling with fear and anger.

The headless figure remained silent. Instead, it went on with its mechanical dance as if it hadn't heard anything I said. My hand shook as I reached out and touched it's featureless face—or the lack thereof. It sent shivers down my spine, as a sense of dread and despair seeped into my soul.

Crystal, who was still recovering from her own illness, noticed how much of an impact these nightly encounters were having on me. Dark circles formed under my eyes, and my demeanor grew more tense. She tried to console me, sensing something was wrong, but I refused to tell her the truth.

As I struggled with the relentless torment of these apparitions, I withdrew further into myself, shutting her out. I knew they were a creation of my own mind, the result of some deep-seated mental illness that had taken root within me. But fear and uncertainty had long overshadowed the rational part of my mind.

The headless figures persisted, infiltrating our lives like a disease. They grew in number, bringing more into our world each night. They weren't just consuming my sanity; they were slowly eroding the foundation of my connection with Crystal.

To keep them at bay, I now spent nights in our living room, barricading our front door with our exercise bike and boxes. My sleep-deprived mind played tricks on me, and I would hear their eerie whispers in the darkness even though their mouths never moved.

One agitated night, as I walked from our living room to the bathroom, I discovered a headless figure standing at the foot of our bed, looming over Crystal. I could feel the weight of its presence bearing down on her as it swayed and twitched. I shouted as I ran into the bedroom, swinging and throwing punches through the menacing figure, startling Crystal. She sat up, her eyes wide with terror.

"What happened?" she cried, her voice trembling.

I couldn't put it into words. How could I tell the woman I loved, the woman I was taking care of, that I was losing my grip on reality, that our once-peaceful home had become a haunting place for the faceless and headless?

Instead, I clutched her close, silently vowing to protect her from whatever malevolent force had taken up residence in our lives.

"I'm sorry," I replied, "I was having a bad dream."

As the weeks turned to months, I continued to see Dr. Masters and tell her about my ordeal. I grew tired of the therapy visits and her attempts to treat me, but I clung to the hope that she would have the answers, the solution to rid my life of the faceless and headless.

I considered suicide in my darkest moments of despair. The constant torment of the hallucinations, as well as the fear that they would eventually consume me completely, became too much to bear. But I couldn't do that to Crystal. She was my every breath, the reason for me to bear the unbearable.

I watched as she recovered from her own illness; her strength and fortitude were an inspiration to me. She never stopped loving me and never gave up on the man I used to be. I couldn't let these grotesque apparitions ruin our future together.

So, I persisted, looking for answers and a glimmer of hope in the darkness that had become my reality. The faceless and headless figures remained, but with Dr. Masters unwavering support, I clung to the hope that one day, I would find a way to confront and eliminate my own demons.

THE PSYCHIATRIST

I thought I was well-versed in the complexities of the human mind. As a loving, devoted husband, I spent hundreds of hours studying the DSM-5, keeping an eye on and assisting my wife as she navigated the perilous waters of PTSD-induced flashbacks and psychosis. The walls of our home proudly display my certificates of completion from Penn Foster and Harvard Health Publishing Medical School. I was familiar with the triggers and potential treatments like the back of my hand.

However, nothing could have prepared me for the terrifying descent into my own mind. I was aware of the warning signs and symptoms. I'd seen my wife go through similar agony. She'd wake up in the middle of the night, drenched in sweat, screaming at the horrors that only she saw. I would hold her trembling body in my arms, whispering soothing words and reminding her that the hallucinations she was seeing and hearing were simply byproducts of her trauma. I used my knowledge and expertise to assist her in rationalizing the irrational.

However, when it happened to me, the gap between my knowledge and experience was vast and unforgiving. My educated mind was constantly at odds with the delusional one. I'd read about cognitive distortions, the tricks our minds play on us, but experiencing them firsthand was an entirely different beast. It was as if sinister forces had kidnapped my consciousness and reveled in my misery.

With their silent laughter, these grotesque, headless figures with elongated limbs mocked me. I knew they weren't real and were the result of my disorganized mind, but their presence was oppressive. No amount of logic or education could make them disappear. It was a daily nightmare that teetered on the edge of sanity and insanity.

I clung to the knowledge I had gained over the years, desperately telling myself this was a passing ailment. I was aware of the statistics, the chances of recovery, and the efficacy of various treatments. I repeated those reassuring facts to myself like a mantra, hoping to drown out the commotion of my hallucinations. But the headless figures persisted. They returned my whispers, their voices a cruel parody of mine.

Months had now passed, and I was becoming increasingly desperate. I tried several techniques that I had suggested to my wife; mindful breathing, coloring, the empty chair technique, aroma therapy, listening to music, but the demons in my head refused to leave, their laughter growing louder with each failed attempt to expel them.

Dr. Masters had been watching my decline with increasing concern. She had witnessed my transformation from a confident, unwavering husband to a broken, haunted man. She made a suggestion during one of our video sessions that cut through my despair.

"James," she said, her voice vibrating with concern, "I think it's time for you to see a psychiatrist."

The suggestion made me shudder. Seeking help for my own mental health was never in the cards. I was the one who rescued my wife, assisted her, dissected her struggle, and offered counsel. Dr. Masters, on the other hand, knew me better than anyone else and understood the gravity of my situation.

"You can't do this alone," she insisted. "Your knowledge will only get you so far. A psychiatrist can prescribe medication to help alleviate your symptoms. It's a recovery bridge."

I reluctantly agreed to see the psychiatrist recommended by Dr. Masters. The thought of taking medication was terrifying, but at that point, I was willing to try anything to regain control of my mind. It felt like I was giving up a piece of myself, the part that had always taken pride in understanding the human psyche. But I had to admit that I was not immune to the horrors that could inhabit any mind, regardless of how well-versed in psychology I was.

The appointment day arrived, and I found myself in the virtual waiting room, my resolve fraying at the edges. Dr. Masters had assured me that the psychiatrist was knowledgeable and compassionate. Still, I couldn't shake the feeling that I would be judged, that my "psychological knowledge" would be questioned by my struggle.

When I finally saw the psychiatrist, she listened intently as I described my terrifying experiences. She challenged me, delving into the depths of my trauma and family history. It was both comforting and unsettling to be on the receiving end of a psychiatric relationship, to be the one seeking rather than aiding.

As per the psychiatrist, my hallucinations likely stemmed from a blend of factors: PTSD (Post Traumatic Stress Disorder) due to my violent, abusive childhood, the recent challenging experiences while tending to Crystal, and my in-depth understanding of psychological conditions.

To aid sleep, Hydroxyzine was prescribed, and Metoprolol was added to ease my symptoms. I was conscious of the potential side effects of both medications, especially Metoprolol, which could possibly heighten feelings of depression and confusion as well as induce nightmares and further disrupt sleep patterns.

The psychiatrist listened attentively to my concerns. I wanted to be as honest as possible about the situation. "Doctor, I'm very concerned about the possible side effects of the medication you're about to prescribe. I am my wife's primary caregiver, and any negative effects on me could make it difficult for me to provide the support and care she requires during her recovery."

I glanced at my kitchen window as another shadowy figure danced across the blinds. My conscience was gnawed by the thought of being unable to care for Crystal at a time when she needed me the most. It wasn't just about me; it was about her, our future, and the delicate balance I was attempting to maintain.

The Dr. nodded; her eyes filled with compassion. "I understand your concern, and it's a valid one," she said softly, her voice soothing. "Being a primary caregiver is a huge responsibility, and your wife's well-being is critical.

We must, however, consider the potential benefits of the prescribed medication on your recovery."

I took a deep breath and asked, "Is there no alternative?" I was torn between my duty to myself and the obligation to prioritize Crystal's health. "Something that could reduce my potential risks?"

The Dr. paused to consider my words. "I am happy to discuss alternative treatment options with you, but I want to be clear that the current medication has shown significant promise in cases like yours. Ultimately, the choice is yours. I can write the prescription, and you can choose whether or not to take it."

I felt a mixture of relief and resignation at the end of my session. The road to recovery lay ahead of me, uncertain and intimidating. I had always been the one to offer advice and support, but now it was my turn. My recovery had begun, and all I could hope for was that with time and treatment, I would be able to return to the rational, stable mind I once knew.

The headless, faceless figures remained at bay as I gazed into the sunlight streaming through the kitchen blinds, their laughter fading into the recesses of my consciousness. The psychiatrist sent the prescription to our local pharmacy...I never picked up the medication. I couldn't risk anything possibly intensifying my anguish or interfering with Crystal's care.

HORRIBLE FLASHBACKS

The images haunted me like a relentless storm, an unyielding downpour of memories that refuse to fade. Amongst them, there's one that echoes louder, one that pierces through the fabric of my thoughts, demanding acknowledgment.

It's the day Crystal was plagued by the command hallucinations, telling her to run into oncoming traffic because she no longer deserved to live.

I can still feel the weight of her despair as she stood there, her eyes a tumultuous sea of emotions—confusion, anguish, frustration, and a hint of defeat. Her unconscious decision was a blade slicing through the fragile threads of our shared existence. She was adamant, determined to break free from the suffocating embrace of her fractured reality.

I grabbed her instinctively, desperately trying to grasp what was slipping away. My fingers intertwined with her shirt, a feeble attempt to anchor her to our life together. But she recoiled, a sudden surge of strength fueled by a command hallucination instructing her to escape.

The struggle was fierce, a battle raging within the confines of her mind. Her attempts to break free were met with my stubborn refusal to let go, to relinquish the last strands of hope tethering us together. In that chaotic ballet of conflicting desires, I felt her slipping away, slipping through my fingers like grains of sand.

Her eyes, once filled with love and familiarity, now bore a distant, hollow gaze that pierced through me. It was like holding onto a ghost, a mere echo of the woman I loved. Each moment stretched agonizingly, a heart-wrenching testament to the unraveling of our bond.

The scene replays in my mind like a relentless loop, each iteration etching deeper grooves of anguish into my soul. The sound of her screaming, her fists beating my face, the hysterical look in her eyes—it's a symphony of heartbreak that reverberates through the corridors of my memory.

Still, years later, that night casts a shadow over our interactions. The fear of losing her lingers, an unspoken specter that looms. I maintain a fragile equilibrium, a dance around unspoken wounds that have yet to heal.

I understand her "reasons." I'm fully aware of the command hallucinations she was suffering from. I know the turmoil that led her to that failed attempt to take her life. But understanding doesn't alleviate the ache of loss, nor does it soothe the wounds carved into the fabric of my mind.

The hardest part is not knowing if I'll ever fully grasp the depth of her pain or if I'll ever mend the fractures etched in my heart. It's a haunting uncertainty, a constant companion in the silence that invades our shared spaces.

As I navigate these turbulent waters of memories, I cling to a flicker of hope—that perhaps amidst these shards of brokenness, there's a chance for redemption, for a renewal of what was once whole.

I never anticipated the vivid persistence of those memories. They haunt me, relentless in their return, weaving themselves into every crevice of my thoughts. It's not just the image of her trying to dash into oncoming traffic; it's also the image of her cutting off her hair in that frenzied moment that continues to resurface. Her emotions, raw and unyielding, burned into my psyche. It's as if time hesitates, looping back and replaying that pivotal instant when my world was turned upside down.

I remember the glint of the scissors, an otherwise innocuous household tool turned into a weapon in her trembling hands. She moved with an urgency that was chillingly alien. The strands of hair, once cascading gently over her shoulders, now lay in disarray on the floor. But it wasn't just the hair she severed; it was her repeated stabs to her head that I can't unsee.

Desperation carved its way into my heart as I reached out, a futile attempt to anchor her to the present, to anchor her to us. Her resistance was staggering, a sheer force of will fueled by a frantic desire to obey the voice in her head.

Her eyes, once the windows to her soul, held a distant, haunted look that shattered my resolve. I held on, feeling her struggle against my grip as she fought to break free.

The echoes of that singular moment haunt the space between us, a lingering presence that tugs at the fragile threads of trust binding our connection. The aftermath has left an unsettling residue, casting shadows upon the foundation of our relationship.

Each step feels tentative now, as though a chasm of uncertainty has opened, making it difficult for me to entirely turn away. There's an unspoken fear, a whispering dread that Crystal might slip back into that unsettling state, and I'll find myself facing a chilling scene—an image of her standing there, clutching a knife or a pair of scissors, poised to follow unseen directives. It's a tango of vigilance, an intricate dance where I'm acutely aware, determined never to be caught off guard again, a solemn oath of wedding vows etched into my consciousness.

The echoes of that event rippled through my days. There's an unspoken tension, an undercurrent of unease that surfaces at unexpected moments. An exaggerated startle response has become my unwelcome companion. The slightest unexpected noise or movement jolts me, triggering a cascade of adrenaline, a reflex borne from the trauma of child abuse, and now, from the memory of those days.

I've become acutely aware of her presence, attuned to her every movement. When she enters a room, my breath catches, and my heart quickens, a visceral reaction beyond my control. It's not her fault; she's unaware of the storm she ignites within me with her mere presence. Yet, the struggle to maintain composure becomes a battle I fight silently, a battle against the ghosts of our shared past.

How do I explain this to her without reopening wounds barely scabbed over? How do I convey the weight of these memories without burdening her with the guilt of their existence? These questions remain unspoken, lingering between us like uncharted territory, too treacherous to traverse.

Some days, I feel like an imposter in my own life, a spectator watching from the sidelines, navigating a landscape marred by fragmented recollections. But amidst this turmoil, there's a sliver of hope, a glimmer of resilience that whispers of healing and redemption.

In the depths of my heart, I cling to the belief that the scars of our past won't define our future. Until then, I live with these flashbacks, these vivid imprints etched into the tapestry of my mind, each one a testament to the love that refuses to fade away, even in the face of adversity.

WRESTLING
WITH THE REAPER

In my early-30s, I became a master of controlling the spawning venom simmering beneath the surface of a composed man. A husband - a role I've come to cherish, a role I feared tarnishing with the seething violence churning from within. I wake each day to the echoes of a fury I cannot contain. It's an inferno raging within me, threatening to consume all reason.

Violence and destruction had been my companions for as long as memory served, shadows threading through the fabric of my existence. My war veteran stepfather wore anger like a hat, his voice, a thunderclap; his hands, agents of chaos. I was a child, an unwilling apprentice to his violent legacy.

Now, I am consumed by the idea of revenge against the man who unceremoniously ripped away my livelihood, my dignity, and my sense of worth. My former shop manager—the architect of my downfall—is etched in my mind, his face a canvas for my turbulent emotions.

My former employer, a grotesquely overweight man devoid of empathy or conscience, knew. He knew of the delicate state of my wife's health. He was privy to the intricacies of her medical condition, the fragility of her existence hanging by a thin thread of hope. He knew of my desperate scramble to balance the demands of work and the desperate need to be by her side, to hold her hand through the agonizing journey of her illness.

I entrusted him with the truth and bared my vulnerability as I applied for Family Medical Leave to care for and provide the support she needed in those trying times. And yet, despite his awareness, despite Crystal's suffering, he callously wielded his power, severing the tie of my employment and medical benefits without a shred of remorse.

Now, I find myself consumed by vengeful thoughts; the allure of retribution tantalizingly close. In my darkest moments, I've envisioned myself storming into the office of my former workplace, a harbinger of death. I see the fear in his eyes, the trembling realization of his impending fate. I am both the architect and the executioner of this imagined reckoning.

My nights are the hardest. In the silence of darkness, my mind becomes a theater of torment. I am haunted by vivid, visceral visions—scenarios meticulously crafted where I am the reaper, the agent of righteous retribution. The scenes play out, I witness myself confronting him, a symphony of pent-up rage and despair orchestrated into one singular, catastrophic act.

I've rehearsed the confrontation a thousand times in my mind, each iteration more vivid and terrifying than the last. I've orchestrated a symphony of suffering that would slice through his conscience, mirroring the searing pain my wife and I have endured. I've conjured elaborate schemes, each more detailed than the last, designed to make him taste the bitterness of helplessness that I've swallowed.

I grapple with conflicting emotions, a turmoil that threatens to consume me whole. The urge to confront him, to inflict an amount of suffering commensurate to his actions, is an incessant drumbeat in my mind. It's a mixture of anger, despair, and my deep seeded primal need for retribution.

Over the years, I've struggled to sever the ties binding me to that violent legacy, to purge this poison from my veins. I seek calmness, hoping to soothe the beast

lurking within. Yet, in moments like this, that animal would rear its head, and I struggle with welcoming and embracing my old friend.

But, the image of Crystal, fragile yet resilient, stays in my mind. I see the exhaustion on her face, and I hear the tremor in her voice as she pleads for peace, for me not to embrace the darkness that threatens to consume me.

She, who fights a battle far more significant than any war I could wage against my former employer, anchors me to a semblance of sanity.

Dr. Masters became my confidant, her virtual office a sanctuary where I unburdened the weight of my turmoil. Strategies and coping mechanisms were prescribed as tools to restrain the Lycanthrope.

I embraced them fervently, desperate for the salvation they promised. Yet, the beast remained, a deep-rooted occupant refusing eviction.

The battlefield lay within—a ceaseless skirmish between reason and wrath. Rationality, a frail shield against my onslaught of emotions. How many times had I dug my nails into my legs to stifle the eruption building within? Countless, each victory short-lived as the monster lay dormant, not defeated.

The days stretch into an eternity as I grapple with this torment. Each passing moment is an exercise in restraint, a battle against the primal urge to embrace death, to demand accountability for the pain inflicted upon my wife.

I find solace in moments of respite, in the quietude of our home where I can hold Crystal's hand and feel the warmth of her fragile existence. The scent of her skin, the glow of her caramel complexion, her mere presence reminds me of the fragility of life and the preciousness of every moment we share.

As I navigate this maelstrom of emotions, I cling to the sliver of humanity that remains untainted by the darkness threatening to consume me. I draw strength from my wife, vowing to channel this storm of emotions into a force for good, to carve a path that transcends vengeance and instead champions empathy and understanding.

The road ahead is fraught with uncertainty, the storm within me far from abating. But in the eye of this storm, I find a glimmer of resilience, a determination to navigate this chaos with grace and emerge stronger, not as a vengeful animal but as a beacon of empathy in a world often devoid of it.

MAKING INTERNAL PEACE WITH MY PARENTS

When I said, "I Do" on that beautiful day in 2005, I knew I was committing myself to a lifetime of love and support. What I didn't anticipate was the unforeseen twist that would lead me down a path of profound self-discovery—my wife's battle with mental health.

Watching someone you cherish wrestle with psychosis is a heartbreaking, humbling experience. At first, I grappled with feelings of helplessness and frustration. I yearned to wave a magic wand and make it all better, to erase the shadows that clouded her mind. But mental health doesn't work that way. It's a delicate maze, and each person's journey is unique.

In my quest to be there for her, I found myself navigating uncharted territories of my own emotions. I had to confront my fears, insecurities, and my childhood, parts of myself I had tucked away, deeming them unnecessary baggage in pursuing a picture-perfect life.

I sought solace in educating myself about mental health. As I learned to support Crystal better, I discovered a deeper understanding of my own inner workings. The patience I exercised for her became a mirror reflecting the need for similar tenderness towards myself.

Through her struggles, I learned the art of active listening. I realized that often, the most significant support I could offer wasn't through grand gestures but through simply being present—holding space for her feelings without judgment or trying to fix things.

More profoundly, her experience forced me to look back on the tumultuous journey of my childhood. The flashes of torturous mistreatment reverberated through my memory, each thought revealing a piece of myself I spent years trying to forget.

Violence and abuse were haunting echoes that resonated within the walls of my mind. The impact of those experiences shaped the person I am today, but it took years to assemble the fragments of that shattered puzzle.

I spent decades running through corridors of confusion. Imagine being lost in a mirrored maze where every path seemed to lead to a dead end. Understanding the reasons behind the turmoil was challenging. As a child, I struggled to comprehend why things were the way they were. Questions lingered, and answers seemed elusive.

The echoes of profane shouting, the sting of harsh hands, and the weight of fear formed the walls of my mind. Each turn brought a new challenge, a new trial to navigate. In those moments, hope felt distant, obscured by the towering walls of uncertainty.

Therapy became my sanctuary—a haven where the layers of trauma began to peel away, exposing the raw emotions I buried deep within. It was here that I started unraveling the intricate threads of chaos woven into my upbringing. The pieces didn't fit neatly together, but they began to form a picture—a fractured portrait of a family plagued by inner demons.

My mother and stepfathers were flawed souls, and through the lens of introspection, I glimpsed the possibility of underlying mental illnesses. My first stepfather, Sid, was not around for very long, yet the memory of being water-tortured in the bathtub and then being locked in a closet for hours at a time still bothers me.

My second stepfather, Rock, a Vietnam War veteran, carried the weight of PTSD and haunting flashbacks. It didn't excuse his prejudiced and violent actions, but it painted a poignant picture of a man shattered by his past, struggling to find peace in the present.

Rock stood as a stark embodiment of the aftermath of war. As a Vietnam veteran, he carried with him the invisible scars of combat, the weight of PTSD pressing down on his shoulders. His haunted eyes spoke volumes, carrying the weight of experiences he couldn't articulate, etched with memories that seemed to replay like a relentless highlight reel. The echoes of war manifested in violent flashbacks, jolting him out of the present into a battlefield long gone. Those moments were raw and heartbreaking, witnessing someone trapped in a reality that blended past horrors with the present. It was a testament to the relentless grip of trauma, an unshakable specter casting shadows over his every action.

His struggles were no excuse for the prejudice and violence that often punctuated my life. Yet, through the lens of empathy, I glimpsed the poignant portrait of a man shattered by his past, struggling to navigate the present. The war he fought seemed to rage on within him, shaping his perceptions and actions in painful and perplexing ways.

I grappled with conflicting emotions—a mixture of resentment for the turmoil he brought into my life and a profound sadness for the demons he battled daily.

Understanding his struggles didn't erase the pain he caused, but it painted a more intricate picture of the complexities within him.

There's a bittersweet understanding that now softens the edges of my memories. I harbor no resentment toward him; instead, I wish his era hadn't stigmatized therapy. Perhaps, with the right help, he could have found solace amidst his turmoil.

My mother, too, was a victim of her history—a cycle of abuse that spanned generations. Her deep-seated hatred for my father, paired with a special hatred in her heart for African American women, stemmed from her own painful experiences.

I learned of my heritage through a chance meeting with my African American family, a reunion that rewrote chapters of my life story.

Discovering my African American roots was a revelation—a meeting with a younger brother, long unknown, who became a bridge to my past. His mother unfolded my parents' high school years, revealing a tale marred by jealousy and bitterness. My birth, marked by a darker complexion resembling my father, inadvertently became a lightning rod for my mother's unresolved anger and prejudices.

Learning about this facet of my past was more than a mere unveiling of facts—it was a journey into understanding the interplay of emotions and the intricate web woven by the past. It was a profound reckoning with the intertwined narratives of race, identity, and the enduring impact of unresolved family conflicts.

Yet, in this discovery, I found a sense of closure. Understanding the tangled web of my mother's trauma, compounded by her own history of abuse, allowed me to release the burden of resentment. The empathy I now hold for her echoes a wish for her to have received the therapy she desperately needed.

For over four decades, these unresolved fragments of my past simmered within, silently shaping my worldview and relationships. Making peace with this chapter required confronting uncomfortable truths, accepting the flawed humanity of those who hurt me, and recognizing the cyclical nature of trauma.

Crystal's journey became intertwined with mine, and in caring for her, I was caring for us. Therapy wasn't just a tool for healing; it became a compass guiding me through the maze of my past, leading me toward forgiveness and self-understanding.

This journey hasn't been easy, but it has been transformative. It taught me that love isn't about fixing someone; it's about standing by them while they heal themselves. And in doing so, I found healing within myself—a peace that stemmed from embracing the complexities of life and the depths of love.

Mental health doesn't discriminate. It doesn't care about age, gender, or social status. But what it does offer, amidst its challenges, is an opportunity—to become better versions of ourselves, to deepen our understanding of compassion and to cherish the moments of joy amidst the storm.

GOD

January 2023, I found myself sitting across my computer screen from Dr. Masters, feeling a mix of vulnerability and relief. It wasn't easy recounting the whirlwind of events that had shattered our lives. Her voice was calm, a steady presence that somehow made the turmoil easier to articulate.

She told me something I hadn't fully accepted: I'd faced an overwhelming amount of stress in such a short time while bearing the weight of caring for my wife. It was as if she felt the invisible burden I carried, the weight of responsibility and love converging into an emotional storm.

Then came her pivotal question: "How did you get through it all? What gave you the strength to keep going?" It was a simple query, but its weight was immense. There was a moment, a long pause filled with memories, as I stared back at the screen, processing the enormity of her question. And then, almost instinctively, His name came out: "God."

I could vividly recall that moment three years ago, the chilling fear coursing through my veins when my wife went missing. Paramedics had taken her to the hospital after a terrifying flashback, a state of psychosis that spiraled her into chaos. But even as law enforcement placed her under a 51/50 hold, the hospital inexplicably let her go.

Before that turmoil, I couldn't remember the last time I prayed. For quite some time I had questioned the existence of God and doubted the validity of faith until that harrowing incident jolted me awake.

I searched frantically, scouring every corner of our city, desperation clinging to every breath as I sought her, but it was a futile hunt. Returning home, defeated and broken, I called the police and filed a missing person report; and then, in the silence that followed, I found myself bowing my head in prayer.

It felt like an ancient, forgotten ritual. I begged for forgiveness. For neglecting that connection, for reaching out to God only in dire need. Tears streamed down my face as I pleaded for her safety, for Him to watch over her, for her safe return. I made a promise, a vow made in desperation and sincerity, that I would love and care for her with my every breath if only she could be brought back to me.

The emptiness of that moment was profound, the agony of uncertainty hanging heavy in the air. And then, as if the heavens heard, a glimmer of hope emerged. Hours later, through the kitchen window, I saw Crystal stumbling up the driveway, disoriented yet alive. In a state of psychosis, but alive. God had answered.

The covenant was made: to care for her at all costs. That was my end of the deal, and I kept it. Pulling her out of the hospital, treading through her mental health struggles, financial hardships, and the loss of stability, all while holding onto love and devotion—that was the manifestation of God's strength within me.

Sharing this with Dr. Masters, I saw tears glistening in her eyes. Her response stunned me, "For the first time in my 33 years of practice, I'm speechless. That was the most beautiful thing I've ever heard a husband say about his wife."

At that moment, I realized the power of faith and the unwavering strength it bestowed upon me in the face of impossible odds. It was a testament to love, resilience, and the unshakeable bond between two souls weathering life's fiercest storms.

CONCLUSION

Here I sit, surrounded by a whirlwind I never anticipated. Life tossed me into this chaotic storm, leaving me grasping for sanity. But amid this, I've encountered the source of this rollercoaster—a revelation that blindsided me, hitting harder than I ever imagined.

PTSD—post-traumatic stress disorder. Those words cast a heavy shadow, a weight I associated mainly with war veterans or my wife's journey. Yet, to hear it applied to my life was an unexpected twist. Questions surged, overwhelming my thoughts, but slowly, a puzzle formed, unraveling how I arrived here.

Caregiver stress is an element I've come to understand deeply, something that can silently sprout from witnessing or experiencing a traumatic event. Its reach spans from combat experiences to natural disasters, from assaults to abuse. Yet, at its core, it leaves a lingering helplessness and terror behind it.

As Dr. Masters explained, my own PTSD had quietly brewed since childhood, an unwanted relic from a past I'd never truly reckoned with. My upbringing was far from nurturing—a battlefield of verbal abuse, physical torture, violence and neglect all chronicled in my first book, "In Love with My 5 Wives, A Broken Man's Journey on How to Love His Broken Wife."

That environment shaped me into a perpetually anxious and violent individual, expecting the worst at every turn. As I grew older, I tried burying those feelings and memories deep, hoping they'd vanish. Instead, they festered, waiting to resurface.

It all erupted in agony, intertwined with my wife's struggles with depression, PTSD, and psychosis. I became her caretaker in a reality twisted beyond recognition. Walking through that hell, witnessing her suffering tormented me, chipping away at my mental well-being.

The stress of caregiving, coupled with the helplessness of easing her pain, brewed a storm within me. Each day felt like an invisible battle. Her cries woke me, and her agony weighed on me till sleep came, an endless cycle of despair.

Then the day arrived when I lost my job—a guillotine severing my stability. I couldn't shield my wife; she sensed the impending catastrophe. Homelessness was never a word I imagined in my life. Evicted, our lives packed into boxes with nowhere to go. The stress of impending homelessness and caring for my wife became an overwhelming weight, unknowingly disconnecting me from reality.

Amid this chaos emerged caregiver stress, a silent foe creeping upon those supporting loved ones with chronic illnesses. It manifests as exhaustion, depression, anxiety, and withdrawal—echoes of my experience.

In focusing entirely on her needs, I forgot my own. I became an empty shell, drained by her care, losing myself in the storm. Recognizing the signs was crucial—nightmares, flashbacks, constant tension, intrusive thoughts—chains linking me to a haunting past.

Dr. Masters' diagnosis marked the first step in understanding this decades-long storm. PTSD and depression had taken root, demanding confrontation. Therapy became my path, navigating this internal tempest. It's been arduous, peppered with setbacks, yet moments of hope surface. I walk this intricate healing journey guided by Dr. Masters and anchored by my wife's unwavering love.

Caregiver stress still lurks, waiting to pounce, but I've learned to spot its warnings and seek aid. It's a battle not just for me but for the woman who steadied me in this storm. Reflecting on the turbulent journey, it all makes sense—the unresolved childhood trauma, the strain of caring for my wife, and the loss of home and job—all culminated, threatening to consume me.

In the quiet moments, as I sit by her side, I find myself reflecting on the unspoken language of love. Caring for my wife, my best friend, on this beautiful journey called life has been a privilege and a challenge I never expected. The weight of responsibility, the daily routines intertwined with worry, and the unrelenting demand for patience often leave me exhausted.

There's an unspoken rhythm between us now. Though it may falter at times, her smile remains the beacon that guides me through the long hours and sleepless nights. Amidst the trials, I've learned that caregiving isn't solely about physical tasks—it's a profound emotional journey where resilience, compassion, and self- care intersect.

Caregiver stress can be overwhelming. There are days when frustration threatens to overshadow the love that binds us. Yet, in the depths of my fatigue, I find solace in the simple moments—the gentle touch of her hand, the faint whisper of her laughter, and the shared memories that transcend our present challenges.

I've learned to find strength in vulnerability. It's okay to admit that this journey is demanding and that the weight on my shoulders sometimes feels insurmountable. Seeking support doesn't diminish my dedication; it amplifies my capacity to care.

God, and therapy have become pillars of resilience, offering guidance and understanding when the weight becomes too much to bear alone.

Self-care, though often neglected, has become non-negotiable. I've learned that taking a moment for myself doesn't equate to ignoring Crystal's needs. It's a crucial act of preservation, enabling me to return with renewed patience and love.

But amidst the chaos, there's beauty too. It's in the way Crystal's eyes light up when I enter the room, in the shared laughter over simple joys, in the resilience that grows within us both as we navigate this uncharted territory.

Though tested by the trials of illness and caregiving, the love we share remains steadfast. It's a love that transcends limitations and has found its strength in adversity.

And so, I choose to embrace each day with gratitude. I am grateful for the chance to care for the woman who has always been my anchor, my friend, confidante, and love. I've come to understand that within the depths of caregiver stress lies an opportunity to deepen our bond, celebrate resilience, and redefine the meaning of unconditional love.

In caring for her, I've discovered a strength within myself I never knew existed. It's a strength borne out of love, compassion, and unwavering dedication—a strength that continues to guide me through the complexities of caregiving, one moment at a time.

At 49, I persist, sharing my story to educate, build and encourage other men. Caregiver stress, PTSD, and depression don't define me. I'm not a victim; I'm a warrior. Raised in darkness and forged for battle. I'll continue fighting these demons, plowing a path toward healing and resilience. Each day, I inch closer to the light, untangling this storm within.

www.ingramcontent.com/pod-product-compliance
Lightning Source LLC
Chambersburg PA
CBHW060240030426
42335CB00014B/1541